GH00835895

POWER

OF CHRIST

THE
POWER AND SYMPATHY
OF CHRIST

EXPOSITORY THOUGHTS, WITH NOTES,
ON THE ELEVENTH CHAPTER OF
ST JOHN'S GOSPEL

J. C. Ryle

'The heart of the wise is in the house of mourning.'
—Eccles. 7:4.

THE BANNER OF TRUTH TRUST

THE BANNER OF TRUTH TRUST

Head Office
3 Murrayfield Road
Edinburgh
EH12 6EL
UK

North America Sales
PO Box 621
Carlisle
PA 17013
USA

banneroftruth.org

This edition © The Banner of Truth Trust 2018

Originally published as a separate book in 1889 under the title
Bethany, its contents first appeared in Ryle's *Expository Thoughts
on the Gospel of St John*, vol. 2, in 1869.

*

ISBN
Print: 978 1 84871 850 0
EPUB: 978 1 84871 851 7
Kindle: 978 1 84871 853 1

*

Typeset in 11/15 Adobe Garamond Pro
at The Banner of Truth Trust, Edinburgh

Printed in the USA by
Versa Press Inc.,
East Peoria, IL.

Contents

Preface

THE book now in the reader's hands requires a few introductory words of explanation. It is an extract from a large expository work in three volumes on the whole Gospel of St John which I put forth about sixteen years ago;[1] a work which, from its size, is not likely to fall into the hands of many readers.

The eleventh chapter of St John occupies such a peculiarly isolated position, and the subjects which are treated in it are of such infinite importance to all professing Christians, that I venture to think that my exposition of the chapter may be found useful and interesting to many in its present separate and detached form.

We are all born to trouble as the sparks fly upwards. We live in a dying world, and 'nightly pitch our moving

[1] J. C. Ryle, *Expository Thoughts on the Gospel of St John*, the first volume of which was originally published in 1865, with volumes 2 and 3 following in 1869 and 1873 respectively. Seven volumes of *Expository Thoughts on the Gospels* were produced by Ryle (Matthew, Mark, Luke, 2 vols, and John, 3 vols). These have been reprinted by the Banner of Truth Trust in a new edition (Edinburgh, 2012).

tent a day's march nearer home'. Year after year the gaps in our family circles increase. Heaven seems to become more full, and earth more empty. Can we begin too soon to look steadily at such great subjects as sorrow, sickness, death, the grave, and the power and sympathy of Christ? I think not.

J. C. LIVERPOOL
Palace, Liverpool
April 22, 1889

CHAPTER ONE

John 11:1-6

1 Now a certain man was sick, named Lazarus, of Bethany, the town of Mary and her sister Martha.

2 (It was that Mary which anointed the Lord with ointment, and wiped his feet with her hair, whose brother Lazarus was sick.)

3 Therefore his sisters sent unto him, saying, Lord, behold, he whom thou lovest is sick.

4 When Jesus heard that, he said, This sickness is not unto death, but for the glory of God, that the Son of God might be glorified thereby.

5 Now Jesus loved Martha, and her sister, and Lazarus.

6 When he had heard therefore that he was sick, he abode two days still in the same place where he was.

THE chapter we have now begun is one of the most remarkable in the New Testament. For grandeur and simplicity, for pathos and solemnity, nothing was ever written like it. It describes a miracle which is not recorded in the other Gospels,—the raising of Lazarus from the dead. Nowhere shall we find such convincing proofs of our Lord's divine power. As God, he makes the grave itself yield up its tenants.—Nowhere shall we find such striking illustrations of our Lord's ability to sympathize with his people. As man, he can be touched with the feeling of our infirmities.—Such a miracle well became the end of such a ministry. It was meet and right that the victory of Bethany should closely precede the crucifixion at Calvary.

These verses teach us that *true Christians may be sick and ill as well as others.* We read that Lazarus of Bethany was one 'whom Jesus loved', and a brother of two well-known holy women. Yet Lazarus was sick, even unto death! The Lord Jesus, who had power over all diseases, could no doubt have prevented this illness, if he had thought fit. But he did not do so. He allowed Lazarus to be sick, and in pain, and weary, and to languish, and suffer, like any other man.

The lesson is one which ought to be deeply graven in our memories. Living in a world full of disease and death, we are sure to need it some day. Sickness, in the very nature of things, can never be anything but trying to flesh and blood. Our bodies and souls are strangely linked together, and that which vexes and weakens the body can hardly fail to vex the mind and soul. But sickness, we must always remember, is no sign that God is displeased with us: nay, more, it is generally sent for the good of our souls. It tends to draw our affections away from this world, and to direct them to things above. It sends us to our Bibles, and teaches us to pray better. It helps to prove our faith and patience, and shows us the real value of our hope in Christ. It reminds us betimes that we are not to live always, and tunes and trains our hearts for our great change. Then let us be patient and cheerful when we are laid aside by illness. Let us believe that the Lord Jesus loves us when we are sick no less than when we are well.

These verses teach us, secondly, that *Jesus Christ is the Christian's best friend in the time of need*. We read that when Lazarus was sick, his sisters at once sent to Jesus, and laid the matter before him. Beautiful, touching, and simple was the message they sent. They did not ask him to come at once, or to work a miracle, and command the disease to depart. They only said, 'Lord, he whom thou lovest is sick', and left the matter there, in the full belief that he would do what was best. Here was the true faith and humility of saints! Here was gracious submission of will!

The servants of Christ, in every age and climate, will do well to follow this excellent example. No doubt when those whom we love are sick, we are to use diligently every reasonable means for their recovery. We must spare no pains to obtain the best medical advice. We must assist nature in every possible manner to fight a good fight against its enemy. But in all our doing, we must never forget that the best and ablest and wisest Helper is in heaven, at God's right hand. Like afflicted Job, our first action must be to fall on our knees and worship. Like Hezekiah, we must spread our matters before the Lord. Like the holy sisters at Bethany, we must send up a prayer to Christ. Let us not forget, in the hurry and excitement of our feelings, that none can help like him, and that he is merciful, loving, and gracious.

These verses teach us, thirdly, that *Christ loves all who are true Christians*. We read that 'Jesus loved Martha, and her sister, and Lazarus.' The characters of these three good people seem to have been somewhat different. Of Martha, we are told in a certain place, that she was 'careful and troubled about many things', while Mary 'sat at Jesus' feet, and heard his word'. Of Lazarus, we are told nothing distinctive at all. Yet all these were loved by the Lord Jesus. They all belonged to his family, and he loved them all.

We must carefully bear this in mind in forming our estimate of Christians. We must never forget that there are varieties in character, and that the grace of God does not cast all believers into one and the same mould. Admitting fully that the foundations of Christian character are always the same, and that all God's children repent, believe, are holy, prayerful, and Scripture-loving, we must make allowances for wide varieties in their temperaments and habits of mind. We must not undervalue others because they are not exactly like ourselves. The flowers in a garden may differ widely, and yet the gardener feels interest in all. The children of a family may be curiously unlike one another, and yet the parents care for all. It is even so with the church of Christ. There are degrees of grace, and varieties of grace; but the least, the weakest, the feeblest disciples, are all loved by the Lord Jesus. Then let no believer's heart fail because of his infirmities and, above all, let no believer dare to despise and undervalue a brother.

These verses teach us, lastly, that *Christ knows best at what time to do anything for his people*. We read that 'when he had heard … that [Lazarus] was sick, he abode two days still in the same place where he was'. In fact, he purposely delayed his journey, and did not come to Bethany till Lazarus had been four days in the grave. No doubt he knew well what was going on: but he never moved till the time came which he saw was best. For the sake of the church and the world, for the good of friends and enemies, he kept away.

The children of God must constantly school their minds to learn the great lesson now before us. Nothing so helps us to bear patiently the trials of life as an abiding conviction of the perfect wisdom by which everything around us is managed. Let us try to believe not only that all that happens to us is well done, but that it is done in the best manner, by the right instrument, and at the right time. We are all naturally impatient in the day of trial. We are apt to say, like Moses, when beloved ones are sick, 'Heal her *now*, O God, I beseech thee' (Num. 12:13). We forget that Christ is too wise a Physician to make any mistakes. It is the duty of faith to say, 'My times are in thy hand. Do with me as thou wilt, how thou wilt, what thou wilt, and when thou wilt. Not my will, but thine be done.' The highest degree of faith is to be able to wait, sit still, and not complain.

Let us turn from the passage with a settled determination to trust Christ entirely with all the concerns of this world, both public and private. Let us believe that he by whom all things were made at first is he who is managing all with perfect wisdom. The affairs of kingdoms, families, and private individuals, are all alike overruled by him. He chooses all the portions of his people. When we are sick, it is because he knows it to be for our good: when he delays coming to help us, it is for some wise reason. The hand that was nailed to the cross is too wise and loving to smite without a needs-be, or to keep us waiting for relief without a cause.

Notes on John 11:1-6

The raising of Lazarus, described in this chapter, is one of the most wonderful events recorded in the Gospels, and demands more than ordinary attention. In no part of our Lord's history do we see him so distinctly both man and God at the same time: man in sympathy, and God in power. Like each of the few incidents in our Lord's ministry related by St John, it is placed before us with peculiar minuteness and particularity. The story is singularly rich in delicate, tender, and beautiful expressions. Before entering upon it, I venture to offer the following preliminary remarks.

(a) The raising of Lazarus was manifestly intended to supply the Jews with one more incontrovertible proof that Jesus was the Christ of God, the promised Messiah. In the tenth chapter, at the feast of dedication, our Lord had been asked, 'If thou be the Christ, tell us plainly' (John 10:24). In reply he had distinctly appealed to his 'works', as the best evidence of his Messiahship. He had deliberately challenged attention to those works as witnesses to his commission. And now, after a short interval, we find him for the last time, within two miles of Jerusalem, before many eye-witnesses, doing such a stupendous work of divine power that a man might have thought any sceptic would have been silenced for ever. After the raising of Lazarus, the Jews of Jerusalem at any rate could never say that they were left destitute of proofs of Christ's Messiahship.

(*b*) The raising of Lazarus was meant to prepare the minds of the Jews for our Lord's own resurrection. It took place between Christmas and Easter, and probably within two months of his own crucifixion. It proved incontrovertibly that a person dead four days could be raised again by divine power, and that the restoration to life of a corpse was not an impossibility with God. I think it impossible not to see in this a latent design to prepare the minds of the Jews for our Lord's own resurrection. At any rate it paved the way for men believing the event to be not incredible. No one could say on Easter Sunday, when the grave of Jesus was found empty, and the body of Jesus was gone, that his resurrection was an impossibility. The mere fact that between winter and Easter in that very year a man dead four days had been restored to life within two miles of Jerusalem, would silence such remarks. Though improbable, it could not be called impossible.

(*c*) The raising of Lazarus is of all our Lord's miracles the one which is most thoroughly credible, and supported by most incontrovertible evidence. The man who disbelieves it may as well say plainly that he does not believe anything in the New Testament, and does not allow that a miracle is possible. Of course there is no standing-ground between denying the possibility of miracles, and denying the existence of a creating God. If God made the world, he can surely change the course of nature at any time, if he thinks fit.

The famous sceptic, Spinoza, declared that if he could be persuaded of the truth of the miracle before us, he would forsake his own system, and embrace Christianity. Yet it is extremely difficult to see what evidence of a fact a man can desire, if he is not satisfied with the evidence that Lazarus really was raised from the dead. But, unhappily, none are so blind as those who will not see.

The following passage from Tittman, the German commentator, is so sensible that I make no apology for giving it at length, though somewhat condensed. 'The whole story', he says, 'is of a nature calculated to exclude all suspicion of imposture, and to confirm the truth of the miracle. A well-known person of Bethany, named Lazarus, falls sick in the absence of Jesus. His sisters send a message to Jesus, announcing it; but while he is yet absent Lazarus dies, is buried, and kept in the tomb for four days, during which Jesus is still absent. Martha, Mary, and all his friends are convinced of his death. Our Lord, while yet remaining in the place where he had been staying, tells his disciples in plain terms that he means to go to Bethany, to raise Lazarus from the dead, that the glory of God may be illustrated, and their faith confirmed. At our Lord's approach, Martha goes to meet him, and announces her brother's death, laments the absence of Jesus before the event took place, and yet expresses a faint hope that by some means Jesus might yet render help. Our Lord declares that her brother shall be raised again, and assures her that he has the power of granting life to the dead. Mary approaches, accompanied by weeping friends from Jerusalem. Our Lord himself is moved, and weeps, and goes to the sepulchre, attended by a crowd. The stone is removed. The stench of the corpse is perceived. Our Lord, after pouring forth audible prayer to his Father, calls forth Lazarus from the grave, in the hearing of all. The dead man obeys the call, comes forth to public view in the same dress that he was buried in, alive and well, and returns home without assistance. All persons present agree that Lazarus is raised to life, and that a great miracle has been worked, though not all believe the person who worked it to be the Messiah. Some go away and tell the rulers at Jerusalem what Jesus has done. Even these do not doubt the truth of the fact; on the contrary, they confess that our Lord by his works is becoming every day more famous, and that he would probably be soon received as Messiah by the whole nation. And *therefore* the rulers at once take counsel how they may put to death both Jesus and Lazarus. The people, in the meantime hearing of this prodigious transaction, flock in multitudes to Bethany, partly to see Jesus, and partly to view Lazarus. And the consequence is that by and by, when our Lord comes to Jerusalem, the population goes forth in crowds to meet him and show him honour, and chiefly because of his work at Bethany. Now if all these circumstances do not establish the truth of the miracle, there is no truth in history.' I only add the remark, that when we consider the place, the time, the circumstances, and the singular publicity of the raising of Lazarus, it really seems to require more credulity to deny it than to believe it. It is the unbeliever, and not the believer of this miracle, who seems to me the credulous man. The difficulties of disbelieving it are far greater than those of believing it.

(*d*) The raising of Lazarus is not mentioned by Matthew, Mark, and Luke. This has stumbled many persons. Yet the omission of the story is not hard to explain. Some have said that Matthew, Mark, and Luke purposely confine themselves to miracles done in Galilee.—Some have said that when they wrote their Gospels Lazarus was yet alive, and the mention of his name would have endangered his safety.—Some have said that it was thought better for the soul of Lazarus not to draw attention to him and surround him with an unhealthy celebrity till after he had left the world.—In each and all of these reasons there is some weight. But the best and simplest explanation probably is, that each Evangelist was inspired to record what God saw to be best and most suitable. No one, I suppose, imagines that the Evangelists record a tenth part of our Lord's miracles, or that there were not other dead persons raised to life, of whom we know nothing at all. 'The dead are raised up', was our Lord's own message, at an early period of his ministry, to John the Baptist (Matt. 11:5). If the works that Jesus did 'should be written every one …,' says John, 'the world itself could not contain the books that should be written' (John 21:25). Let it suffice us to believe that each Evangelist was inspired to record exactly those events which were most likely to be profitable for the church in studying his Gospel. Our Lord's ministry and sayings at Jerusalem were specially assigned to John. What wonder then that he was appointed to record the mighty miracle which took place within two miles of Jerusalem, and proved incontrovertibly the guilt of the Jerusalem Jews in not receiving Jesus as the Messiah?

Bucer remarks, that there is a continually ascending great-ness and splendour in those miracles which John was inspired to record in his Gospel, and that the raising of Lazarus was the most illustrious of all. He also observes that our Lord specially chose the great feasts at Jerusalem as occasions of working miracles.

Chemnitius remarks, 'There is not in the whole Evangelical narrative a more delightful history, and one more abundant both in doctrine and consolation, than this of the raising of Lazarus. It therefore ought to be studied most closely and minutely by all pious minds.'

1.—Now a certain man … sick … Lazarus.

These simple words are the keynote to the whole chapter. All turns on the bodily illness of an obscure disciple of Christ. How much in the history of our lives hinges on little events, and specially on illnesses! Sickness is a sacred thing, and one of God's great ordinances.

This illness took place between winter and Easter, during the time that our Lord was at Bethabara, beyond Jordan. The nature of the disease we are not told; but from its rapid course, it is not unlikely it was a fever, such as is common even now in Palestine.

This is the first time that Lazarus is mentioned in the New Testament, and we know nothing certain of his history. Some have conjectured that he was the young ruler who came to our Lord, asking what he must do to obtain eternal life, and went away sorrowful at the time, but was afterwards converted.—Some have conjectured that he is the young man who followed our Lord when he was taken prisoner, mentioned by St Mark, and fled away naked.—But these are mere guesses, and there is really no solid foundation for them. That he was not a poor man, but comparatively rich, seems highly probable from the 'feast' in John 12, the number of friends who came to mourn him, the alabaster box of precious ointment used by his sister, and the sepulchre hewn out of rock. But even this is only a conjecture.

The name 'Lazarus' no doubt is a Greek form of the Hebrew name 'Eleazar'. It is worth noticing, that it survives to this day in the modern name of Bethany: 'El-Azarizeh'. (See *Smith's Biblical Dictionary*.)

Of Bethany ... town of Mary ... Martha.

The word 'town' in this sentence would have been better translated 'village', as it is in sixteen other texts in the New Testament. Bethany, in truth, was only a small village, a short two miles from Jerusalem, on the east side; and its situation is perfectly known now. It lies on the eastern slope of the Mount of Olives, on the road to Jericho. It is not once mentioned in the Old Testament, and owes its fame to its being the place where Lazarus was raised,—the place where our Lord rested at night just before the passion,—the place from which he commenced his triumphant entry into Jerusalem,—the place from which he finally ascended into heaven (Luke 24:50, 51), and the dwelling-place of Mary and Martha.

Let it be noted that the presence of God's elect children is the one thing which makes towns and countries famous in God's sight. The village of Martha and Mary is noticed, while Memphis and Thebes are not named in the New Testament. A cottage where there is grace, is more pleasant in God's sight than a cathedral town where there is none.

Let it be noted that this verse supplies internal evidence that St John's Gospel was written long after the other historical parts of the New Testament. He speaks of Martha and Mary as persons whose names and history would be familiar to all Christian readers.

There is a peculiarity in the Greek of this verse, which is hardly conveyed in our English translation. Literally it would be rendered, 'Lazarus *from* Bethany, *out of* the town of Mary', etc. That 'from' Bethany means exactly what we render it, is clear from Acts 17:13; Hebrews 13:24. But why 'out of the village, or town of Mary' is said, is not quite so clear. It is open to the conjecture that it may mean 'Lazarus was now a man of Bethany, but was originally out of the town of Mary and Martha': viz., some other place. But this seems unlikely.— Webster suggests that 'out of' is added by way of emphasis, to show that Lazarus not only lived there, but that it was also the place of his nativity. Greswell says much the same. It is noteworthy that John 1:44 contains exactly the same form of expression about Philip and Bethsaida.

It is noteworthy that Mary is named before Martha, though Martha was evidently the older sister, and head of the house. The reason, I suppose, is that Mary's name and character were better known of the two.

Chemnitius thinks it possible that all Bethany belonged to Martha and Mary, and that this accounts for the consideration in which they were held, and the number of mourners, etc. It is worth remembering that Bethany was a very small place. Yet Bethsaida was called the 'city of Andrew and Peter' (John 1:44), and clearly did not belong to two poor fishermen.

2.—*It was that Mary, etc.*

This verse is a parenthetical explanation inserted by St John after his manner, to make it certain what Mary he refers to, as the sister of Lazarus. Christians knew there were in our Lord's time no less than four Marys: (1) The virgin mother of our Lord, (2) the wife of Cleopas, (3) Mary Magdalene, (4) Mary the sister of Martha. To prevent, therefore, any mistake, John says, 'It was that Mary who anointed our Lord, whose brother Lazarus was dead.'

Simple as these words seem, there is a singular diversity of opinion as to the question who Mary the sister of Martha and Lazarus was, and how many times our Lord was anointed.

(*a*) Some, as Chrysostom, Origen, and Chemnitius, maintain that the anointing took place three times: once, in Luke 7, at the house of Simon the Pharisee; once in Bethany, at the house of Simon the leper; and once in Bethany, at the house of Martha and Mary. Others, as Ferus, while agreeing with Chrysostom that our Lord was anointed three times, think Mary was the woman who twice did it.

(*b*) Some maintain that our Lord was anointed twice: once at the Pharisee's house (in Luke 7), and once at Bethany, at the house of Simon the leper (Mark 14:3), where Martha and Mary and Lazarus lived, for some cause which we do not know.

(*c*) Some, as Augustine, Bede, Toletus, Lightfoot, Maldonatus, Cornelius à Lapide, and Hengstenberg, maintain that our Lord was only once anointed,—that the narrative in Luke 7 was inserted out of chronological order,—that Simon the Pharisee and Simon the leper were the same person, and that the one anointing took place at Bethany. Hengstenberg supports this theory very ingeniously, and boldly suggests that Simon the Pharisee was also called Simon the leper, was the husband of Martha, and not friendly to Christ; that this accounts for Martha being more 'careful and troubled' (in Luke 10:41) than Mary, and for unfriendly Pharisees being present at the raising of Lazarus; that Mary Magdalene was the same as Mary of Bethany,—and that Mary of Bethany was the 'sinner' in Luke 7.

Toletus frankly admits that the Romish Church holds that there was only one anointing by one person, as it is plainly declared in one of her formularies: viz., the Breviary.

My own opinion is decidedly against the last of these views. I hold that there were *at least* two anointings; one at a comparatively early period of our Lord's ministry, and another at the close of it,—one in the house of an unfriendly Pharisee named Simon, and another at the house of Simon the leper, in Bethany,—one by a woman who had been pre-eminently a sinner, another by Mary the sister of Martha, against whose moral character we know nothing.—Why the house of Martha and Mary at Bethany is called the house of Simon the leper, I admit I cannot explain. I can only surmise that there was some relationship of which we know nothing. But this difficulty is nothing in my eyes, compared to that of supposing, with Augustine and his followers, that the event described in Luke 7 took place just at the end of our Lord's ministry. There is strong internal evidence that it did not, to my mind. Surely at the end of our Lord's ministry, people would not have said with wonder, 'Who is this that forgiveth sins?' Surely Mary would not be spoken of as a notorious 'sinner'.

On the other hand, if we hold the view that our Lord was only anointed twice,—once at the house of Simon the Pharisee, and once at Bethany,—it must be frankly admitted that there is a very grave difficulty to be got over. That difficulty is that St Mark says that a woman anointed our Lord 'two days' before the passover, and poured the ointment on his 'head', while John says he was anointed 'six days before the passover', and the ointment poured on his 'feet'.—I do not see how this difficulty can be got over.

If however we hold that our Lord was anointed twice in the last week before he was crucified, once 'six days' before, and once 'two days' before, and on each occasion by a woman, the whole thing is clear. That such a thing should be done more than once, in those days, does not strike me as any objection, considering the customs of the age. That our Lord's language in defence of the woman should on each occasion be the same is somewhat remarkable. But it is only a minor difficulty. On the whole therefore, if I must give an opinion, I incline to agree with Chrysostom, that there were three anointings. I also think there is something in the view of Ferus, that Mary, sister of Lazarus, anointed our Lord twice,—once six days before the passover, and once again two days before.

The use of the past participle in the verse before us seems to me no difficulty at all. It is of course true that at this time Mary had not anointed our Lord. But it is no less true that John evidently mentions it by anticipation, as a historical fact long past and well known in the church when he wrote his Gospel, which his readers would understand. 'It was that Mary which afterwards anointed Christ's feet.'

Let us note in this verse, that the good deeds of all Christ's saints are carefully recorded in God's book of remembrance. Men are forgetful and ungrateful. Nothing done for Christ is ever forgotten.

Let us note that sickness comes to Christ's people as well as to the wicked and worldly. Grace does not exempt us from trial. Sickness, on the contrary, is one of God's most useful instruments for sanctifying his saints, and making them bear fruit of patience, and for showing the world that his people do not serve him merely for what they get of bodily ease and comfort in this life. 'Job does not serve God for nought', was the devil's sneer, in the days when Job prospered. 'Lazarus and his sisters make a good thing of their religion',—might have been said if they had had no trials.

Brentius remarks, 'God does not go away when bodily health goes away. Christ does not depart when life departs.'

3.—Therefore his sisters sent … saying.

This is an example of what all Christians should do in trouble. Like Mary and Martha, we should first send a message to Christ. By prayer we can do it as really as they did. This is what Job did in his trouble: he first of all 'worshipped', and said, 'Blessed be the name of the LORD.' This is what Asa did not do: 'He sought not to the LORD, but to the physicians' (Job 1:20, 21; 2 Chron. 16:12).

Let it be noted that the Greek would be more literally rendered 'the sisters', and not 'his'. This message, from the expression in the next verse, 'heard', would seem to have been a verbal and not a written one.

Lord … he whom thou lovest is sick.

This is a very touching and beautiful little message.—Its humble and respectful confidence is noteworthy: 'He whom thou lovest is sick.' They do not say, 'Do something', or 'Heal him', or 'Come at once.' They simply spread the case before the Lord, and leave him to do what he thinks wisest and best. It is like Hezekiah spreading Sennacherib's letter before God (2 Kings 19:14).—The name given to Lazarus is noteworthy: they do not say 'our brother', or 'thy disciple', or even 'one who loves thee', but simply 'he whom thou lovest'; one whom thou hast been pleased to treat graciously and kindly as a beloved friend. Christ's love to us, and not our love to Christ, is the blessed truth which we ought continually to keep before our minds. His love never changes: ours is wavering and uncertain.

The idea of some, that sending a message to Christ was a mark of weak faith in the two sisters, as if it showed doubt of Christ's omniscience, is absurd. At this rate we might never pray, and might say there is no need, because God knows all!

The word 'behold' seems either to indicate something 'sudden' in the illness of Lazarus, like Mark 2:24, and to be used adverbially; or else we must take it as an imperative verb. 'Behold a case of great affliction: look upon it and see. He whom thou lovest is sick.' This would be like Hezekiah's prayer: 'Open ... thine eyes, and see' (2 Kings 19:16). We can hardly suppose that such disciples as Martha and Mary would think it a strange or surprising thing that a disciple of Christ should be ill; yet it is possible they did. However, Theophylact and Ferus suppose that 'behold' implies a degree of wonder and surprise.

Rupertus remarks, on the message containing no request: 'To a loving friend it was quite enough to announce the fact that Lazarus was sick.' Affectionate friends are not verbose or lengthy in descriptions.

Brentius remarks that the message is like all true prayer: it does not consist in much speaking, and fine long sentences.

Musculus and Chemnitius both remark, that when a man's child falls into a well or pit, it is enough to tell a loving father the simple fact, in the shortest manner possible, without dwelling on it verbosely and rhetorically.

Rollock observes how useful it is to have praying sisters.

Let us note that Christ's friends may be sick and ill, just like other people. It is no proof that they are not beloved, and specially preserved and cared for by God. 'Whom the Lord loveth he chasteneth.' The purest gold is most in the fire; the most useful tools are oftenest ground. Epaphroditus and Timothy were both of weak health, and Paul could not prevent it.

4.—When Jesus heard that, he said.

This verse seems to contain the reply which our Lord gave to the messenger. It was to him probably, though in the hearing of all his disciples, that he addressed the words which follow. It is as though he said, 'Go, return to thy mistress, and say as follows.'

This sickness is not unto death, etc.

The meaning of this sentence must evidently be taken with qualification. Our Lord did not mean that Lazarus would not in any sense die. It is as though he said, 'The end of this sickness is not Lazarus' death and entire removal from this world, but generally the glory of God, and specially the glorifying of me, his Son, which will be effected by my raising him again.' Death's temporary victory over us is not complete till our bodies perish and return to dust. This was not allowed in the case of Lazarus, and hence death had not full dominion over him, though he ceased to breathe and became unconscious.

It is undeniable that there was something dark and mysterious about our Lord's message. He might of course have said plainly, 'Lazarus will die, and then I will raise him again.' Yet there is a wonderful likeness between the style of his message and many an unfulfilled prophecy. He said enough to excite hope, and encourage faith and patience and prayer, but not enough to make Mary and Martha leave off praying and seeking God. And is not this exactly what we should feel about many an unfulfilled prediction of things to come? Men complain that prophecies are not so literally fulfilled as to exclude doubt and uncertainty. But they forget that God wisely permits a degree of uncertainty in order to keep us watching and praying. It is just what he did with Martha and Mary here.

Let us remember that the final result of Lazarus' sickness is what we should desire as the result of any sickness that comes on us and our families: viz., that God and Christ may be glorified in us. We cannot say, 'It shall not end in death'; but we can say, 'By God's help, it shall be for God's glory.'

Chrysostom observes, 'The expression *that* in this passage denotes not cause but consequence. The sickness happened from other causes. Christ used it for the glory of God.'

Calvin remarks, that God wishes to be honoured by Christ being glorified. He who does not honour the Son does not honour the Father (John 5:23).

5.—*Now Jesus loved Martha, etc.*

This verse is meant to show that all the members of the family at Bethany were disciples of Jesus and beloved by him, the brother as well as the sisters, and one sister as well as the other. A happy family, Lampe remarks, in which all the members were objects of Christ's special love!

We know not where Lazarus was at the time when Jesus stopped at Martha's house, in Luke 10:38; perhaps he was not converted at that time. But this is only conjecture.

We are generally apt to undervalue the grace of Martha and overvalue that of Mary, because of what happened when Jesus was at Martha's house before. Many foolish things are sometimes lightly said against mothers and mistresses as being Marthas, 'careful and troubled about many things'. Yet people should remember that different positions call out different phases of character. Mary certainly shines more brightly than Martha in chapter 10 of Luke; but it is a grave question whether Martha did not outshine her in chapter 11 of John. Active-minded Christians come out better under some circumstances; quiet-minded Christians, in others. Our Lord teaches us here that he loves all who have grace, though their temperaments differ. Let us learn not to judge others rashly, and not to form hasty estimates of Christians, until we have seen them under every sort of circumstances, in winter as well as summer, in dark days as well as bright.

Let it be noted that the Greek word here rendered 'loved', is not the same that is rendered 'lovest', in verse 3. The word describing the love of Jesus to the three in this verse is a word expressing a high, deep, excellent, and noble affection. It is the same as Mark 10:21, and John 3:16.—The word used in the message of the sisters, is a lower word, such as is used to describe the affection between a parent and child, or husband and wife. It is the word used for 'kiss' in Matthew 26:48; Mark 14:44; and Luke 22:47. It is very noticeable that this word is carefully avoided here, when the two sisters are mentioned. The Holy Ghost inspired John to abstain even from the appearance of evil. What a lesson this ought to be to us!

Let it be noted that we see here an example of the broad distinction that ought to be drawn between Christ's general love of compassion which he feels towards all mankind, and his special love of election which he feels towards his own members. He loved all sinners to whom he came to preach the gospel, and he wept over unbelieving Jerusalem. But he specially loved those who believed on him.

6.—When he had heard therefore, etc.

It is impossible not to remark an intentional and most instructive connection between this verse and the preceding one. Our Lord loved the family of Bethany, all three of them; and yet when he heard Lazarus was sick, instead of hastening at once to Bethany to heal him, he quietly remained at Bethabara for two days, without moving.

We cannot doubt that this delay was intentional and of purpose, and it throws immense light on many of God's providential dealings with his people. We know that the delay caused immense mental pain and suffering to Martha and Mary, and obliged Lazarus to go through all the agony of death, and the sorrow of parting. We can easily imagine the grief and suspense and perplexity in which the household at Bethany must have been kept for four days, when their loving Master did not appear; and we know that our Lord could have prevented it all, but did not. But we know also that if he had at once hurried to Bethany and healed Lazarus, or spoken a word from a distance at Bethabara and commanded his healing, as in John 4:50, the mighty miracle of raising him would never have been wrought, and the wonderful sayings of Bethany would never have been spoken. In short, the pain of a few was permitted for the benefit of the whole church of Christ.

We have here the simplest and best account of the permission of evil and suffering. God could prevent it. God does not love to make his creatures suffer. But God sees there are lessons which mankind could not learn unless evil was permitted: therefore God permits it. The suffering of some tends to the good of many. 'He that believeth shall not make haste' (Isa. 28:16). We shall see at the last day that all was well done. Even the delays and long intervals which puzzle us in God's dealings, are wisely ordered, and are working for good. Like children, we are poor judges of half-finished work.

Chrysostom says, 'Christ tarried that none might be able to assert that he restored Lazarus when not yet dead, saying it was a lethargy, a fainting, a fit, but not death. He therefore tarried so long that corruption began.'

Calvin observes, 'Let believers learn to suspend their desires, if God does not stretch out his hand to help as soon as they think necessity requires. Whatever may be his delays, he never sleeps, and never forgets his people.'

Quesnel remarks, 'God permits evil, that he may make the power of his grace and the might of his love more conspicuous in the conversion of a sinner.'

Poole remarks, 'We must not judge of Christ's love to us by his mere external dispensations of providence, nor judge that he doth not love us, because he doth not presently come in to our help at our time, and in such ways and methods as we think reasonable.'

CHAPTER TWO

John 11:7-16

7 Then after that saith he to his disciples, Let us go into Judæa again.

8 His disciples say unto him, Master, the Jews of late sought to stone thee; and goest thou thither again?

9 Jesus answered, Are there not twelve hours in the day? If any man walk in the day, he stumbleth not, because he seeth the light of this world.

10 But if a man walk in the night, he stumbleth, because there is no light in him.

11 These things said he: and after that he saith unto them, Our friend Lazarus sleepeth; but I go, that I may awake him out of sleep.

12 Then said his disciples, Lord, if he sleep, he shall do well.

13 Howbeit Jesus spake of his death: but they thought that he had spoken of taking of rest in sleep.

14 Then said Jesus unto them plainly, Lazarus is dead.

15 And I am glad for your sakes that I was not there, to the intent ye may believe; nevertheless let us go unto him.

16 Then said Thomas, which is called Didymus, unto his fellow-disciples, Let us also go, that we may die with him.

WE should notice, in this passage, *how mysterious are the ways in which Christ sometimes leads his people.* We are told that when he talked of going back to Judæa, his disciples were perplexed. It was the very place where the Jews had lately tried to stone their Master. To return thither was to plunge into the midst of danger. These timid Galileans could not see the necessity or prudence of such a step. 'Goest thou thither again?' they cried.

Things such as these are often going on around us. The servants of Christ are often placed in circumstances just as puzzling and perplexing as those of the disciples. They are led in ways of which they cannot see the purpose and object; they are called to fill positions from which they naturally shrink, and which they would never have chosen for themselves. Thousands in every age are continually learning this by their own experience. The path they are obliged to walk in is not the path of their own choice. At present they cannot see its usefulness or wisdom.

At times like these, a Christian must call into exercise his faith and patience. He must believe that his Master knows best by what road his servant ought to travel, and that he is leading him, by the right way, to a city of habitation. He may rest assured that the circumstances in which he is placed are precisely those which are most likely to promote his graces and to check his besetting sins. He need not doubt that what he cannot see now he will understand hereafter. He will find one day that there was wisdom in every step of his journey, though flesh and blood could not see it at the time. If the twelve disciples had not been taken back into Judæa, they would not have seen the glorious miracle of Bethany. If Christians were allowed to choose their own course through life, they would never learn hundreds of lessons about Christ and his grace, which they are now taught in God's ways. Let us remember these things. The time may come when we shall be called to take some journey in life which we greatly dislike. When that time comes, let us set out cheerfully, and believe that all is right.

We should notice, secondly, in this passage, *how tenderly Christ speaks of the death of believers*. He announces the fact of Lazarus being dead in language of singular beauty and gentleness: 'Our friend Lazarus sleepeth.'

Every true Christian has a Friend in heaven, of almighty power and boundless love. He is thought of, cared for, provided for, defended by God's eternal Son. He has an unfailing Protector, who never slumbers or sleeps, and watches continually over his interests. The world may despise him, but he has no cause to be ashamed. Father and mother even may cast him out, but Christ having once taken him up will never let him go. He is the 'friend of Christ' even after he is dead! The friendships of this world are often fair-weather friendships, and fail us like summer-dried fountains, when our need is the sorest; but the friendship of the Son of God is stronger than death, and goes beyond the grave. The Friend of sinners is a Friend that sticketh closer than a brother.

The death of true Christians is 'sleep', and not annihilation. It is a solemn and miraculous change, no doubt, but not a change to be regarded with alarm. They have nothing to fear for their souls in the change, for their sins are washed away in Christ's blood. The sharpest sting of death is the sense of unpardoned sin. Christians have nothing to fear for their bodies in the change: they will rise again by and by, refreshed and renewed, after the image of the Lord. The grave itself is a conquered enemy. It must render back its tenants safe and sound, the very moment that Christ calls for them at the last day.

Let us remember these things when those whom we love fall asleep in Christ, or when we ourselves receive our notice to quit this world. Let us call to mind in such an hour, that our great Friend takes thought for our bodies as well as for our souls, and that he will not allow one hair of our heads to perish. Let us never forget that the grave is the place where the Lord himself lay, and that as he rose again triumphant from that cold bed, so also shall all his people. To a mere worldly man death must needs be a terrible thing; but he that has Christian faith may boldly say, as he lays down life, 'I will ... lay me down in peace, and sleep: for thou, LORD, only makest me dwell in safety' (Psa. 4:8).

We should notice, lastly, in this passage, *how much of natural temperament clings to a believer even after conversion.* We read that when Thomas saw that Lazarus was dead, and that Jesus was determined, in spite of all danger, to return into

Judæa, he said, 'Let us also go, that we may die with him.' There can only be one meaning in that expression: it was the language of a despairing and desponding mind, which could see nothing but dark clouds in the picture. The very man who afterwards could not believe that his Master had risen again, and thought the news too good to be true, is just the one of the twelve who thinks that if they go back to Judæa they must all die!

Things such as these are deeply instructive, and are doubtless recorded for our learning. They show us that the grace of God in conversion does not so re-mould a man as to leave no trace of his natural bent of character. The sanguine do not altogether cease to be sanguine, nor the desponding to be desponding, when they pass from death to life, and become true Christians. They show us that we must make large allowances for natural temperament, in forming our estimate of individual Christians. We must not expect all God's children to be exactly one and the same. Each tree in a forest has its own peculiarities of shape and growth, and yet all at a distance look one mass of leaves and verdure. Each member of Christ's body has his own distinctive bias, and yet all in the main are led by one Spirit, and love one Lord. The two sisters Martha and Mary, the Apostles Peter and John and Thomas, were certainly very unlike one another in many respects. But they had all one point in common: they loved Christ, and were his friends.

Let us take heed that we really belong to Christ. This is the one thing needful. If this is made sure, we shall be led by the right way, and end well at last. We may not have the cheerfulness of one brother, or the fiery zeal of another, or the gentleness of another. But if grace reigns within us, and we know what repentance and faith are by experience, we shall stand on the right hand in the great day. Happy is the man of whom, with all his defects, Christ says to saints and angels, 'This is our friend.'

NOTES ON JOHN 11:7-16

7.—Then after that saith ... disciples.

The Greek words which begin this sentence mark an interval of time even more emphatically than our English version does. They would be literally rendered, 'Afterwards, after this.' The word translated 'then' is the same that is translated 'after that' in 1 Corinthians 15:6, 7.

Let us go ... Judæa again.

This is the language of the kind and loving head of a family, and the chief in a party of friends. Our Lord does not say, 'I shall go to', or, 'Follow me to Judæa', but, 'Let us go.' It is the voice of a kind Master and Shepherd proposing a thing to his pupils and followers, as though he would allow them to express their opinions about it. How much depends on the manner and language of a leader!

The familiar, easy manner in which our Lord is said here to tell his disciples what he proposes to do, gives a pleasant idea of the terms on which they lived with him.

8.—His disciples say … Master.

The answer of the disciples is an interesting illustration of the easy terms on which they were with their Master. They tell him frankly and unreservedly their feelings and fears.

Let it be noted that the word rendered 'Master' here is the well-known word 'Rabbi'. The use of it shows that there is nothing necessarily insulting, sneering, or discourteous about the term. It was the title of honour and respect given by all Jews to their teachers. Thus John the Baptist's disciples said to him, when jealous for his honour, 'Rabbi, he that was with thee', etc. (John 3:26).

The Jews of late sought to stone thee.

The 'Jews' here means especially the leaders or principal persons among the scribes and Pharisees at Jerusalem, as it generally does in St John's Gospel. The word rendered 'of late' is generally translated 'now', or 'at this time'. There is not another instance of its being translated 'of late' in the New Testament. Hence the sentence would be more literally rendered, 'The Jews even now were seeking to stone thee.' They allude to the attempt made at the feast of dedication a few weeks before. The attempt was so recent that it seemed 'even now'.

And goest thou thither again?

This question indicates surprise and fear.—'Do we hear aright? Dost thou really talk of going back again to Judæa? Dost thou not fear another assault on thy life?'—We can easily detect fear for their own safety, as well as their Master's, in the question of the disciples: yet they put it on 'thee', and not on 'us'.

Let us note how strange and unwise our Lord's plans sometimes appear to his short-sighted people. How little the best can understand his ways!

9, 10.—*Jesus answered, Are there not twelve hours? etc.*

The answer which our Lord makes to the remonstrance of his timid disciples is somewhat remarkable. Instead of giving them a direct reply, bidding them not to be afraid, he first quotes a proverbial saying, and then draws from that saying general lessons about the time which anyone who is on a journey will choose for journeying. He draws no conclusion, and leaves the application to be made by the disciples themselves. To an English ear the answer seems far more strange than it would to an Eastern one. To quote a proverb is, even now, a common reply among Orientals. To fill up the sense of our Lord's elliptical reply, and draw the conclusions he meant to be drawn, but did not express, is, however, not very easy. The following may be taken as a paraphrase of it:—

'Are not the working hours of the day twelve? You know they are, speaking generally. If a man on a journey walks during these twelve daylight hours, he sees his road, and does not stumble or fall, because the sun, which is the light of the world, shines on his path. If, on the contrary, a man on a journey chooses to walk in the unreasonable hour of night, he is likely to stumble or fall, for want of light to guide his feet. It is even so with me. My twelve hours of ministry, my day of work, is not yet over. There is no fear of my life being cut off before the time: I shall not be slain till my work is done. Till mine hour is come, I am safe, and not a hair of my head can be touched. I am like one walking in the full light of the sun, and cannot fall. The night will soon be here when I shall walk on earth no longer: but the night has not yet come. There are twelve hours in my day of earthly ministry, and the twelfth with me has not arrived.'

This seems to me substantially the correct explanation of our Lord's meaning. The idea of ancient writers, as Hugo and Lyranus, that our Lord meant, by mentioning the twelve hours of the day, that men often change their minds as the day goes on, and that the Jews, perhaps, no longer wished to kill him, is very improbable and unsatisfactory.

I grant that the conclusion of the tenth verse, 'there is no light in him', presents some difficulty. The simplest explanation is, that it only means, 'because he has no light'.

Pearce conjectures that the clause should be rendered, 'Because there is no light in it: viz., the world.' The Greek will perhaps bear this interpretation.

Let us note that the great principle underlying the two verses is the old saying in another form, 'Every man is immortal till his work is done.' A recollection of that saying is an excellent antidote against fears of danger. The missionary in heathen lands, and the minister at home, pressed down by unhealthy climate, or over-abundant work, may take comfort in it, after their Lord's example. Let us only, by way of caution, make sure that our dangers meet us in the path of duty, and that we do not go out of the way to seek them.

Rupertus suggests that our Lord had in his mind his own doctrine, that he was the light and sun of the world. Now as the sun continues shining all the twelve hours of the day, and no mortal power can stop it, so he would have the disciples know that until the evening of his own course arrived, no power of the Jews could possibly check, arrest, or do him harm. As to the disciples, he seems to add, 'So long as I am shining on you with my bodily presence, you have nothing to fear, you will not fall into trouble. When I am taken from you, and not till then, you will be in danger of falling into the hands of persecutors, and even of being put to death.' Œcolampadius takes the same view.

Melanchthon thinks that our Lord uses a proverbial mode of speech, in order to teach us the great broad lesson that we must attend to the duties of our day, station, and calling, and then leave the event to God. In the path of duty all will turn out right. Calvin, Bullinger, Gualter, and Brentius, take much the same view.

Leigh remarks, 'Christ comforts from God's providence. God made the day twelve hours. Who can make it shorter? Who can shorten man's life?'

Does it not come to this, that our Lord would have the disciples know that he himself could not take harm till his day of work was over, and that they could take no harm while he was with them? (Compare Luke 13:32, 33.) Bishop Ellicott suggests that this was the very time in our Lord's ministry when he said to the Pharisee, 'I do cures today and tomorrow, and the third day I shall be perfected. Nevertheless I must walk today and tomorrow and the day following.' But I doubt this.

It is certain that there came a time when our Lord said, 'This is your hour, and the power of darkness', to his enemies. Then he was taken, and his disciples fled.

11.—These things … Our friend Lazarus sleepeth.

In this verse our Lord breaks the fact that Lazarus is dead to his disciples. He does it in words of matchless beauty and tenderness. After saying 'these things' about the twelve hours of the day, which we have considered in the last verse, he seems to make a slight pause. Then, 'after that', comes the announcement which would be more literally rendered, 'Lazarus, the friend of us, has been laid asleep.'

The word 'sleepeth' means, 'is dead'. It is a gentle and pathetic way of expressing the most painful of events that can befall man, and a most suitable one, when we remember that after death comes resurrection. In dying we are not annihilated. Like sleepers, we lie down, to rise again. Estius well remarks, 'Sleeping, in the sense of dying, is only applied to men, because of the hope of the resurrection. We read no such thing of brutes.'

The use of the figure is so common in Scripture, that it is almost needless to give references (see Deut. 31:16; Dan. 12:2; Matt. 27:52; Acts 7:60; 13:36; 1 Cor. 7:39; 11:30; 15:6, 18; 1 Thess. 4:13, 14). But it is a striking fact that the figure is frequently used by great heathen writers, showing clearly that the tradition of a life after death existed even among the heathen. Homer, Sophocles, Virgil, and Catullus, supply instances. However, the Christian believer is the only one who can truly regard death as sleep,—that is, as a healthy, refreshing thing, which can do him no harm. Many among ourselves, perhaps, are not aware that the figure of speech exists among us in full force in the word 'cemetery', applied to burial ground. That word is drawn from the very Greek verb which our Lord uses here. It is literally a 'sleeping place'.

The word 'friend', applied to Lazarus, gives a beautiful idea of the relation between the Lord Jesus and all his believing people. Each one is his 'friend',—not servant, or subject only, but 'friend'. A poor believer has no cause to be ashamed. He has a Friend greater than kings and nobles, who will show himself friendly to all eternity. A dead saint lying in the grave is not cut off from Christ's love: even in his grave, he is still the friend of Christ.

The expression 'our', attached to friend, teaches the beautiful lesson that every friend of Christ is or should be the friend of all Christians. Believers are all one family of brothers and sisters, and members of one body. Lazarus was not 'my' friend, but 'our' friend. If anyone is a friend of Christ, every other believer should be ready and willing to hold out his hand to him, and say, 'You are my friend.'

When our Lord says, 'I go that I may awake him out of sleep', he proclaims his deliberate intention and purpose to raise Lazarus from the dead. He boldly challenges the attention of the disciples, and declares that he is going to Bethany, to restore a dead man to life. Never was bolder declaration made. None surely would make it but One who knew that he was very God.

'I go' is equivalent to saying, 'I am at once setting forth on a journey to Bethany.' The expression 'that I may awake him out of sleep' is one word in Greek, and is equivalent to 'that I may unsleep him'. What our Lord went to do at Bethany, he is soon coming to do for all our friends who are asleep in Christ. He is coming to awaken them.

Some commentators have thought that Lazarus died in the very moment that our Lord said, 'Our friend sleepeth', and that it means, 'Lazarus has just fallen asleep and died.' But this is only conjecture, though doubtless our Lord knew the moment of his decease.

Let it be noted that our Lord says, 'I go', in the singular number, and not 'Let us go.' Does it not look as if he meant, 'Whether you like to go or not, I intend to go'?

Hall remarks, 'None can awaken Lazarus out of this sleep, but he that made Lazarus. Every mouse or gnat can raise us up from that other sleep; none but an omnipotent power from this.'

12.—Then said … disciples … sleep … well.

It seems strange that the disciples should misunderstand our Lord's words, considering how commonly death was called sleep. But their unwillingness to go into Judæa probably made them shut their eyes to our Lord's real meaning.

Most writers think that the disciples referred to the general opinion, that sleep in a sickness is a sign of amendment. Some, however, suggest that they had gathered from the messenger sent by Martha and Mary what was the precise nature of Lazarus' illness, and therefore knew that it was one in which sleep was a favourable symptom.

The Greek word for 'he shall do well' is curious. It is the same that is often rendered, 'shall be made whole'. Sometimes it is 'healed', and generally 'saved'.

The latent thought is manifest: 'If Lazarus sleeps, he is getting better, and there is no need of our going to Judæa.'

13.—Howbeit Jesus spake, etc.

This verse is one of those explanatory glosses which St John frequently puts into his narrative parenthetically. The three first words of the verse would be more literally rendered, 'But Jesus had spoken.'

How the disciples could have 'thought' or 'supposed' that our Lord meant literal sleep, and not death, seems strange, when we remember that Peter, James, and John, had heard him use the same expression after the death of the ruler's daughter: 'The maid … sleepeth' (Matt. 9:24). Two probable

THE POWER AND SYMPATHY OF CHRIST

reasons may be assigned:—one is that they had heard from the messenger that Lazarus' recovery turned on his getting sleep, and that if he only got some sleep he might do well; the other is that they were so afraid of returning to Judæa, that they determined to believe Lazarus was getting better, and to construe our Lord's words in the way most agreeable to their fears. It is common to observe that men will not understand what they do not want to understand.

Quesnel remarks here, 'The misunderstanding of the apostles was a great instance of stupidity, and shows plainly how sensual and carnal their minds still were. The knowledge of this is useful in order to convince incredulous persons that the apostles were not of themselves capable either of converting the world, or of inventing the wonderful things and sublime discourses which they relate.'

The readiness of the disciples to misunderstand figurative language is curiously shown in two other places, where our Lord spoke of 'leaven' and 'meat' (Matt. 16:6, 7; John 4:32, 33).

14.—*Then said Jesus … plainly, Lazarus is dead.*

Here at last our Lord breaks the fact of Lazarus' death to his disciples openly, and without any further reserve. He had approached the subject gently and delicately, and thus prepared their minds for something painful, by steps. First he said simply, 'Let us go into Judæa', without assigning a reason. Secondly he said, 'Lazarus sleepeth.' Lastly he says, 'Lazarus is dead.' There is a beautiful consideration for feelings in these three steps. It is a comfortable thought that our mighty Saviour is so tender-hearted and gentle. It is an instructive lesson to us on the duty of dealing gently with others, and specially in announcing afflictions.

38

The word rendered 'plainly' is the same as in John 10:24. Here, as there, it does not mean 'in plain, intelligible language', so much as 'openly, unreservedly, and without mystery'.

15.—And I am glad … not there … believe.

This sentence would be more literally rendered, 'And I rejoice on account of you, in order that ye may believe, that I was not there.' Our Lord evidently means that he was glad that he was not at Bethany when Lazarus became ill, and had not healed him before his death, as in all probability he would have done. The result now would be most advantageous to the disciples. Their faith would receive an immense confirmation, by witnessing the stupendous miracle of Lazarus being raised from the dead. Thus great good, in one respect, would come out of great evil. The announcement they had just heard might be very painful and distressing, but he, as their Master, could not but be glad to think how mightily their faith would be strengthened in the end.

Let us note that our Lord does not say, 'I am glad Lazarus is dead', but 'I am glad I was not there.' Had he been there, he seems to say, he could not have refused the prayer of Martha and Mary, to heal his friend. We are not intended to be so unfeeling as to rejoice in the death of Christian friends: but we may rejoice in the circumstances attending their deaths, and the glory redounding to Christ, and the benefit accruing to saints from them.

Let us note that our Lord does not say, 'I am glad for the sake of Martha and Mary and Lazarus that I was not there', but 'for your sakes'. It is no pleasure to him to see his individual members suffering, weeping, and dying; but he does rejoice to see the good of many spring out of the suffering of a few. Hence he permits some to be afflicted, in order that many may be instructed through their afflictions. This is the key to the permission of evil in the world: it is for the good of the many. When we ourselves are allowed of God to suffer, we must remember this. We must believe there are wise reasons why God does not come to our help at once and take the suffering away.

Let us note our Lord's desire that his disciples 'may believe'. He did not mean that they might believe now for the first time, but that they might believe more firmly, heartily, and unhesitatingly; that their faith in short might receive a great increase by seeing Lazarus raised. We see here the immense importance of faith. To believe on Christ, and trust God's Word, is the first step towards heaven. To believe more and trust more, is the real secret of Christian growth, progress, and prosperity. To make us believe more is the end of all Christ's dealings with us (see John 14:1).

Nevertheless let us go unto him.

The first word here would be more literally rendered 'But'. It is as though our Lord said, 'But let us delay no longer: let us cast aside all fears of danger; let us go to our friend.'

It is noteworthy that our Lord says, 'Let us go to Lazarus', though he was dead, and would be buried by the time they reached Bethany. Can it be that the disciples thought he had David's words about his dead child in his mind, 'I shall go to him'? The words of Thomas, in the next verse, seem to make it possible.

We may notice three gradations in our Lord's language about going to Bethany. The first, in verse 7: there he says in the plural, 'Let us all go into Judæa.' The second, in verse 11: there he says in the singular, 'I go to awake him': as though he was ready to go alone.—The third is here in the plural, 'Let us all go.'

Toletus thinks that by these words our Lord meant to hint his intention of raising Lazarus.

Burkitt remarks, 'O love, stronger than death! The grave cannot separate Christ and his friends. Other friends accompany us to the brink of the grave, and then they leave us.—Neither life nor death can separate from the love of Christ.'

Bengel remarks, 'It is beautifully consonant with divine propriety, that no one is ever read of as having died while the Prince of Life was present.'

16.—*Then said Thomas ... go ... die with him.*

The disciple here named is also mentioned in John 14:5, and John 20:24-27. On each occasion he appears in the same state of mind,—ready to look at the black side of everything,—taking the worst view of the position, and raising doubts and fears. In John 14:5, he does not know where our Lord is going. In John 20:25, he cannot believe our Lord has risen. Here he sees nothing but danger and death, if his Master returns to Judæa. Yet he is true and faithful nevertheless. He will not forsake Christ, even if death is in the way. 'Let us go', he says to his fellow-disciples, 'and die with our Master. He is sure to be killed if he does go; but we cannot do better than be killed with him.'

Some, as Brentius, Grotius, Leigh, Poole, and Hammond, think that 'with him' refers to Lazarus. But most commentators think that Thomas refers to our Lord: with them I entirely agree.

Let it be noted that a man may have notable weaknesses and infirmities of Christian character, and yet be a disciple of Christ. There is no more common fault among believers, perhaps, than despondency and unbelief. A reckless readiness to die and make an end of our troubles is not grace but impatience.

Let us observe how extremely unlike one another Christ's disciples were. Peter, for instance, overrunning with zeal and confidence, was the very opposite of desponding Thomas. Yet both had grace, and both loved Christ. We must not foolishly assume that all Christians are exactly like one another in details of character. We must make large allowances, when the main features are right.

Let us remember that this same Thomas, so desponding in our Lord's lifetime, was afterwards the very apostle who first preached the gospel in India, according to ecclesiastical history, and penetrated further East than any whose name is recorded. Chrysostom says, 'The very man who dared not go to Bethany in Christ's company, afterwards ran alone through the world, and dwelt in the midst of nations full of murder and ready to kill him.'

Some have thought that his Greek name 'Didymus', signifying 'two' or 'double', was given him because of his character being double: viz., part faith and part weakness. But this is very doubtful. In the first three Gospels, in the catalogue of the twelve, he is always named together with Matthew the publican. But why we do not know.

The Greek word for 'fellow-disciple' is never used in the New Testament excepting here.

CHAPTER THREE

John 11:17-29

17 Then when Jesus came, he found that he had lain in the grave four days already.

18 Now Bethany was nigh unto Jerusalem, about fifteen furlongs off:

19 And many of the Jews came to Martha and Mary, to comfort them concerning their brother.

20 Then Martha, as soon as she heard that Jesus was coming, went and met him: but Mary sat still in the house.

21 Then said Martha unto Jesus, Lord, if thou hadst been here, my brother had not died.

22 But I know, that even now, whatsoever thou wilt ask of God, God will give it thee.

23 Jesus saith unto her, Thy brother shall rise again.

24 Martha saith unto him, I know that he shall rise again in the resurrection at the last day.

25 Jesus said unto her, I am the resurrection, and the life: he that believeth in me, though he were dead, yet shall he live:

26 And whosoever liveth and believeth in me shall never die. Believest thou this?

27 She saith unto him, Yea, Lord: I believe that thou art the Christ, the Son of God, which should come into the world.

28 And when she had so said, she went her way, and called Mary her sister secretly, saying, The Master is come, and calleth for thee.

29 As soon as she heard that, she arose quickly, and came unto him.

T HERE is a grand simplicity about this passage, which is almost spoilt by any human exposition. To comment on it seems like gilding gold or painting lilies. Yet it throws much light on a subject which we can never understand too well: that is, the true character of Christ's people. The portraits of Christians in the Bible are faithful likenesses. They show us saints just as they are.

We learn, firstly, *what a strange mixture of grace and weakness is to be found even in the hearts of true believers.*

We see this strikingly illustrated in the language used by Martha and Mary. Both these holy women had faith enough to say, 'Lord, if thou hadst been here, my brother had not died.' Yet neither of them seems to have remembered that the death of Lazarus did not depend on Christ's absence, and that our Lord, had he thought fit, could have prevented his death with a word, without coming to Bethany.—Martha had knowledge enough to say, 'I know, that even now, whatsoever thou wilt ask of God, God will give it thee … I know that [my brother] shall rise again … at the last day … I believe that thou art the Christ, the Son of God': but even she could get no further. Her dim eyes and trembling hands could not grasp the grand truth that he who stood before her had the keys of life and death, and that in her Master dwelt 'all the fulness of the Godhead bodily' (Col. 2:9). She saw indeed, but through a glass darkly. She knew, but only in part. She believed, but her faith was mingled with much unbelief. Yet both Martha and Mary were genuine children of God, and true Christians.

These things are graciously written for our learning. It is good to remember what true Christians really are. Many and great are the mistakes into which people fall, by forming a false estimate of the Christian's character. Many are the bitter things which people write against themselves, by expecting to find in their hearts what cannot be found on this side of heaven. Let us settle it in our minds that saints on earth are not perfect angels, but only converted sinners. They are sinners renewed, changed, sanctified, no doubt; but they are yet sinners, and will be till they die. Like Martha and Mary, their faith is often entangled with much unbelief, and their grace compassed round with much infirmity. Happy is that child of God who understands these things, and has learned to judge rightly both of himself and others. Rarely indeed shall we find the saint who does not often need that prayer, 'Lord, I believe; help thou mine unbelief' (Mark 9:24).

We learn, secondly, *what need many believers have of clear views of Christ's person, office, and power*. This is a point which is forcibly brought out in the well-known sentence which our Lord addressed to Martha. In reply to her vague and faltering expression of belief in the resurrection at the last day, he proclaims the glorious truth, 'I am the resurrection, and the life';—'I, even I, thy Master, am he that has the keys of life and death in his hands.' And then he presses on her once more that old lesson, which she had doubtless often heard, but never fully realized:—'He that believeth in me, though he were dead, yet shall he live: and whosoever liveth and believeth in me shall never die.'

There is matter here which deserves the close consideration of all true Christians. Many of them complain of want of sensible comfort in their religion. They do not feel the inward peace which they desire. Let them know that vague and indefinite views of Christ are too often the cause of all their perplexities. They must try to see more clearly the great object on which their faith rests. They must grasp more firmly his love and power toward them that believe, and the riches he has laid up for them even now in this world. We are many of us sadly like Martha. A little general knowledge of Christ as the only Saviour is often all that we possess. But of the fulness that dwells in him, of his resurrection, his priesthood, his intercession, his unfailing compassion, we have tasted little or nothing at all. They are things of which our Lord might well say to many, as he did to Martha, 'Believest thou this?'

Let us take shame to ourselves that we have named the name of Christ so long, and yet know so little about him. What right have we to wonder that we feel so little sensible comfort in our Christianity? Our slight and imperfect knowledge of Christ is the true reason of our discomfort. Let the time past suffice us to have been lazy students in Christ's school: let the time to come find us more diligent in trying to 'know him, and the power of his resurrection' (Phil. 3:10). If true Christians would only strive, as St Paul says, to 'comprehend … what is the breadth, and length, and depth, and height; and to know the love of Christ, which passeth knowledge', they would be amazed at the discoveries they would make (Eph. 3:18, 19). They would soon find, like Hagar, that there are wells of water near them of which they had no knowledge. They would soon discover that there is more heaven to be enjoyed on earth than they had ever thought possible. The root of a happy religion is clear, distinct, well-defined knowledge of Jesus Christ. More knowledge would have saved Martha many sighs and tears. Knowledge alone, no doubt, if unsanctified, only 'puffeth up' (1 Cor. 8:1). Yet without clear knowledge of Christ in all his offices we cannot expect to be established in the faith, and steady and unmoved in the time of need.

NOTES ON JOHN 11:17-29

17.—Then when Jesus came.

We are left entirely to conjecture as to the time spent by our Lord in his journey from Bethabara to Bethany. We do not know anything certain of the place where he was abiding, except that it was beyond Jordan. Probably it was between twenty and thirty miles from Bethany, and this distance, to those who travelled on foot, would be at least a day's journey.

He found ... lain ... grave four days already.

The Greek form of language here is peculiar, and a literal translation would be impossible. It would be, 'He found him being already four days in the grave.' It is highly probable that Lazarus was buried the same day that he died. In a country like Palestine, with a hot climate, it is quite impossible to keep corpses long unburied, without danger and discomfort to the living. A man may talk to his friend one day, and find him buried the next day.

One thing is abundantly proved by this verse. Lazarus must certainly have been dead, and not in a trance or swoon. A person lying in a grave for four days, all reasonable people would admit, must have been a dead man.

The various forms of death which our Lord is recorded to have triumphed over should not be forgotten. Jairus' daughter was just dead; the son of the widow of Nain was being carried to the grave; Lazarus, the most extraordinary case of all, had been four days in the tomb.

The expression, 'he found', in this verse, must not be thought to imply any surprise. We know that our Lord began his journey from Bethabara with a full knowledge that Lazarus was dead. What 'he found' applies to Lazarus therefore, and to the precise length of time that he had been in the grave. He was not only dead, but buried.

We can well imagine what a sorrowful time those four days must have been to Martha and Mary, and how many thoughts must have crossed their minds as to the reason of our Lord's delay, as to the day he would come, and the like. Nothing so wears us down as suspense and uncertainty. Yet of all graces there is none so glorifying to God and sanctifying to the heart as that of patience or quietly waiting. How long Abraham, Jacob, Joseph, Moses, and David were kept waiting! Jesus loves to show the world that his people can wait. Martha and Mary had to exemplify this. Well if we can do likewise!

Gomarus discusses at length the curious question, where the soul of Lazarus was during those four days. He dismisses as unscriptural the idea that it was yet in the body, and seems to hold that it was in paradise.

The 'four days' are easily accounted for, if we remember the time occupied by the messenger from Bethany, the two days' delay at Bethabara, and the journey to Bethany.

18.—*Now Bethany was nigh unto Jerusalem, about fifteen furlongs off.*

This verse shows that John wrote for readers who were not acquainted with Palestine. According to his manner he gives a parenthetical description of the situation of Bethany, partly to show how very near to Jerusalem the wonderful miracle he relates was worked,—within a walk of the temple, and almost within view; and partly to account for the number of the Jews who came from Jerusalem to comfort Martha and Mary.

The distance, fifteen furlongs, is rather less than two miles. The use of the expression 'about' shows that the Holy Ghost condescends to use man's common form of language in describing things, and that such expressions are not inconsistent with inspiration (see John 2:6; 6:19).

19.—And many of the Jews came ... Mary.

This sentence would be more literally rendered, 'Many from among the Jews had come to those around Martha and Mary.' Who these Jews were it is impossible to say, except that they evidently came from Jerusalem. One can hardly suppose that they were the leaders and rulers of the Pharisees. Such men would not be likely to care for friends of Jesus, and would hardly have condescended to visit Martha and Mary, who were doubtless known to be his disciples. Of course it is possible that Simon the leper, in whose house Lazarus died, may have been a man of consideration, and that the Jews may have come out of respect to him. At any rate it is clear that those who saw the stupendous miracle of this chapter were Jerusalem Jews, and were 'many', and not few.—The expression, 'Those around Martha and Mary', is a form of language not uncommon in Greek, and is probably rightly translated in our version. It can hardly mean, 'the women who had come to mourn with Martha and Mary', though it is well known that women were the chief mourners at funerals. It is, however, only fair to say that Beza decidedly holds that the women and female friends who had come to mourn with Mary and Martha are meant in this verse.

To comfort them concerning their brother.

This appears to have been a common practice among the Jews. When anyone died, friends and neighbours assembled for several days at the house of the deceased, to mourn with and comfort the relatives. Lightfoot specially mentions it. The same custom prevails in many parts of the world at the present day: Hindostan and Ireland are instances.

We cannot doubt that many of these Jews came to Martha and Mary from form and custom, and not from any genuine sympathy or kind feeling, much less from any unity of spiritual taste. Yet it is striking to observe how God blesses even the semblance of sympathy. By coming they saw Christ's greatest miracle. If unbelief can sympathize, how much more should grace.

One thing at any rate seems very clearly proved by this verse. Whatever was the rank or position of Martha, Mary, and Lazarus, they were well-known people, and anything that happened in their house at Bethany was soon public news in Jerusalem. Had they been strangers from Galilee, the thing named in this verse would not have been written.

Chrysostom thinks the Evangelist mentioned the Jews coming to comfort Martha and Mary, as one of the many circumstances proving that Lazarus was really dead. They evidently thought him dead, or they would not have come.

Lightfoot gives a long and curious account of the customs of the Jews about comforting mourners. He says that 'thirty days were allotted for the time of mourning. The three first days were for weeping; seven days for lamentation; and thirty days for intermission from washing or shaving. The beds in the house of mourning were all taken down and laid on the ground, as soon as the coffin left the house. The comforter sat on the floor; the bereaved sat chief. The comforter might not say a word till the chief mourner broke silence.'

Poole observes that the mourning for Jacob was forty days, for Aaron and Moses, thirty days (Gen. 50:3; Num. 20:29; Deut. 34:8).

20.—*Then Martha … heard that Jesus was coming … met him.*

The Greek word for 'was coming' would have been more literally translated, 'is coming', or, 'comes', in the present tense. It then gives the idea that Martha received from some friend, servant, or watchman, who was on the lookout on the road from Jordan, the message long looked for, 'Jesus is in sight': 'He is coming.' She then hurried out, and met our Lord outside the village. The Greek is simply, 'met him'; and 'went' is needless.

Bullinger thinks that Martha, with characteristic activity, was bustling after domestic duties, and heard from someone that Jesus was coming, and ran to meet him, without going to tell Mary.

But Mary sat still ... house.

While Martha hurried out to meet Jesus, Mary continued sitting in the house. Martha's 'met' is a perfect tense; Mary's 'sat' is an imperfect. It is impossible not to see the characteristic temperament of each sister coming out here, and doubtless it is written for our learning. Martha—active, stirring, busy, demonstrative—cannot wait, but runs impulsively to meet Jesus. Mary—quiet, gentle, pensive, meditative, contemplative, meek,—sits passively at home. Yet I venture to think that of the two sisters, Martha here appears to most advantage. There is such a thing as being so crushed and stunned by our affliction that we do not adorn our profession under it. Is there not something of this in Mary's conduct throughout this chapter? There is a time to stir, as well as to sit still; and here, by not stirring, Mary certainly missed hearing our Lord's glorious declaration about himself. I would not be mistaken in saying this. Both these holy women were true disciples; yet if Mary showed more grace on a former occasion than Martha, I think Martha here showed more than Mary.

Let us never forget that there are differences of temperament among believers, and let us make due allowance for others if they are not quite like ourselves. There are believers who are quiet, passive, silent, and meditative; and believers who are active, stirring, and demonstrative. The well-ordered church must find room, place, and work for all. We need Marys as well as Marthas, and Marthas as well as Marys.

Nothing brings out character so much as sickness and affliction. If we would know how much grace believers have, we should see them in trouble.

Let us remember that 'sitting' was the attitude of a mourner, among the Jews. Thus Job's friends 'sat down with him upon the ground' (Job 2:13).

Henry remarks, 'In the day of affliction Mary's contemplative and reserved temper proved a snare to her, made her less able to grapple with grief, and disposed her to melancholy. It will be our wisdom to watch against the temptations, and improve the advantages of our natural temper.'

21.—*Then said Martha … if thou … not died.*

This is the first account of Martha's feelings. It was the uppermost thought in her mind, and with honest impulsiveness she brings it out at once. It is easy to detect in it a strange mixture of emotions.

Here is passion, not unmixed with a tinge of reproach. 'I wish you had been here: why did you not come sooner? You might have prevented my brother's death.'

Here is love, confidence, and devotion creeping out. 'I wish you had been here. We loved you so much. We depended so entirely on your love. We felt if you had been here all would be ordered well.'

Here is faith. 'I wish you had been here. I believe you could have healed my brother, and kept death from him.'

Nevertheless there is something of unbelief at bottom. Martha forgets that the bodily presence of Jesus was not necessary in order to cure her brother, or to prevent his death. She must have known what our Lord did for the centurion's servant, and the ruler of Capernaum. He had but to speak the word anywhere and Lazarus would have recovered. But memories often fail in time of trouble.

Ferus remarks how apt we all are to say, as Martha, 'If God had been here, if Christ had been present, this would not have happened; as if Christ was not always present, and everywhere near his people!'

Henry remarks that in cases like Martha's, 'we are apt to add to our trouble by fancying what might have been. If such a method had been taken, such a physician employed, my friend had not died! which is more than we know. And what good does it do? When God's will is done, our business is to submit.'

22.—But I know … even now … ask … give it thee.

In these words poor Martha's faith and hope shine clearly and unmistakably, though not without serious blemishes. 'Even now', she says, 'though my brother is dead and lying in the grave, I know, and feel confident, from the many proofs I have seen of thy power, that whatsoever things thou mayest ask of God, God will give them to thee. I must therefore even now cling to the hope that in some way or other thou wilt help us.'

The faith of these words is plain and unmistakable. Martha hopes desperately against hope, that somehow all will be right, though she knows not how. She has strong confidence in the efficacy of our Lord's prayers.

The presence of dim views and indistinct apprehensions of Christ in Martha's mind is as evident as her faith. She speaks as if our Lord was a human prophet only, and had no independent power of his own, as God, to work a miracle, and as if he could not command a cure, but must ask God for it, as Elisha did. She must have strangely forgotten the manner in which our Lord had often worked his miracles. Chrysostom remarks, that she speaks as if Christ was only 'some virtuous and approved mortal'.

Let us note here that there may be true faith and love toward Christ in a person, and yet much dimness and ignorance mixed up with it. Love to Christ, in Christian women especially, is often much clearer than faith and knowledge. Hence women are more easily led astray by false doctrine than men. It is of the utmost importance to remember that there are degrees of faith and knowledge. How small a degree of faith may save, and how much of ignorance may be found even in one who is on the way to heaven, are deep points which probably the last day alone will fully disclose.

Let us do Martha the justice to observe that she shows great confidence in the value and efficacy of prayer.

23.—*Jesus saith … brother shall rise again.*

These words, the first spoken by our Lord after arriving at Bethany, are very remarkable. They sound as if he saw the vague nature of Martha's faith, and would gradually lead her on to clearer and more distinct views of himself, his office, and person. He therefore begins by the broad, general promise, 'Thy brother shall be raised up.' He does not say when or how. If his disciples heard him say this, they might have some clue to his meaning, as he had said, 'I go that I may awake him out of sleep.' But Martha had not heard that.

Let us note that our Lord loves to draw out the faith and knowledge of his people by degrees. If he told us everything at once, plainly, and without any room for misunderstanding, it would not be good for us. Exercise is useful for all our graces.

Rollock sees in this verse a signal example of our Lord's unwillingness to 'break the bruised reed, or quench the smoking flax'. He nourishes and encourages the little spark of faith which Martha had.

24.—*Martha ... I know ... resurrection ... last day.*

Martha here reveals the extent of her faith and knowledge. She knows and feels sure that her brother will be raised again from the dead in the last day, when the resurrection takes place. This, as a pious Jewess, she had learned from the Old Testament Scriptures, and as a Christian believer, she had gathered even more distinctly from the teaching of Jesus. But she does not say, 'I know and feel confident' of anything more. She may perhaps have had some glimmering of hope that Jesus would do something, but she does not say, 'I know that he will.' General faith is easier than particular.

We see from this verse that the resurrection of the body formed part of the creed of the Jewish church, and of the faith of our Lord's disciples. Martha's '*I know*', sounds as if she remembered the words of Job, 'I know that my redeemer liveth.' What she did not understand, or had failed to remember, was our Lord's peculiar office as Lord of the resurrection. We cannot now understand how she can have failed to hear what our Lord had said before the Sanhedrin (John 5:25-29). Very probably she was not at Jerusalem at the time. If she did hear it, she evidently had not comprehended it. Even our

Lord's teaching was often not taken in by his people! How much less must his ministers expect all their sermons to be understood.

To my eyes there is an evident tone of disappointment about Martha's speech. It is as though she said, 'I know, of course, that he will rise again at last; but that is cold comfort. It is a far distant event. I want nearer and better consolation.'

Hutcheson remarks, 'It is no uncommon thing to see men believing great things that are far off, and about which they have no present exercise, when yet their faith proves weak in the matter of a present trial, though less difficult than that which they profess to believe.'

25.—*Jesus said … I am … resurrection … life.*

In this and the following verses, our Lord corrects Martha's feeble and inadequate notions, and sets before her more exalted views of himself. As Chrysostom says, 'He shows her that he needed none to help him.' He tells her that he is not merely a human teacher of the resurrection, but the divine Author of all resurrection, whether spiritual or physical, and the Root and Fountain of all life. 'I am that high and holy One who by taking man's nature upon me, have ennobled his body, and made its resurrection possible. I am the great First Cause and Procurer of man's resurrection, the Conqueror of death, and the Saviour of the body. I am the great Spring and Source of all life, and whatever life anyone has, eternal, spiritual, physical, is all owing to me. All that are raised from the grave will be raised by me. All that are spiritually quickened are quickened by me. Separate from me there is no life at all. Death came by Adam; life comes by me.'

All must feel that this is a deep saying, so deep that we see but a little of it. One thing only is very clear and plain: none could use this language but one who knew and felt that he was very God. No prophet or apostle ever spoke in this way.

I do not feel sure that the two first words of this verse do not contain a latent reference to the great title of Jehovah, 'I am.' The Greek quite permits it.

He that believeth in me ... dead ... live.

This sentence receives two interpretations. Some, as Calvin and Hutcheson, hold that 'dead' here means *spiritually* dead.—Others, as Bullinger, Gualter, Brentius, Musculus, hold that 'dead' means *bodily* dead.—With these last I entirely agree, partly because of the point that our Lord is pressing on Martha, partly because of the awkwardness of speaking of a believer as 'dead'. Moreover, the expression is a verb,—'though he has died', and not an adjective,—'is a dead person'. The sense I believe to be this: 'He that believes in me, even if he has died, and been laid in the grave, like thy brother, shall yet live, and be raised again through my power. Faith in me unites such a one to the Fountain of all life, and death can only hold him for a short time. As surely as I, the Head, have life, and cannot be kept a prisoner by the grave, so surely all my members, believing in me, shall live also.'

26.—*And whosoever liveth ... believeth ... never die.*

In this verse our Lord seems to me to speak of living believers, as in the last verse he had spoken of dead ones. Here, then, he makes the sweeping declaration, that 'everyone who believes in him shall never die': that is, 'he shall not die eternally', as the Burial Service of the Church of England has it. The second death shall have no power over him. The sting of bodily death shall be taken away. He partakes of a life that never ends, from the moment that he believes in Christ. His body may be laid in the grave for a little season, but only to be raised after a while to glory; and his soul lives on uninterruptedly for evermore, and, like the great risen Head, dieth no more.

That there are great depths in this and the preceding sentence, every reverent believer will always admit. We feel that we do not see the bottom. The difficulty probably arises from the utter inability of our gross, carnal natures to comprehend the mysteries of life, death, and resurrection of any kind. One thing is abundantly clear, and that is the importance of faith in Christ. 'He that believeth' is the man who though dead shall live, and shall never die. Let us take care that we believe, and then all shall one day be plain. The simple questions, 'What is life, and what is death?' contain enough to silence the wisest philosopher.

Believest thou this?

This searching question is the application to Martha of the great doctrines just laid down. 'Thou believest that the dead will rise. It is well. But dost thou believe that I am the Author of resurrection, and the source of life? Dost thou realize that I, thy Teacher and Friend, am very God, and have the keys of death and the grave in my hands? Hast thou yet got hold of this? If thou hast not, and only knowest me as a prophet sent to teach good and comfortable things, thou hast only received half the truth.'

Some questions like these are very useful. How little we most of us know what we really believe, and what we do not; what we have grasped and made our own, and what we hold loosely. Above all, how little we know what we really believe about Christ.

Melanchthon points out how immensely important it is to know whether we really have faith, and believe what we hold.

27.—She saith ... Yea, Lord: I believe.

Poor Martha, pressed home with the mighty question of the last verse, seems hardly able to give any but a vague answer. In truth, we cannot expect that she would speak distinctly about that which she only understood imperfectly. She therefore falls back on a general answer, in which she states simply, yet decidedly, what was the extent of her creed.

Our English word, 'I believe', hardly gives the full sense of the Greek. It would be literally, 'I have believed, and do believe.' This is my faith, and has been for a long time.

Augustine, Bede, Bullinger, Chemnitius, Gualter, Maldonatus, Quesnel, and Henry, think that the first word of Martha's reply is a full and explicit declaration of faith in everything our Lord had just said. 'Yes, Lord, I do believe thou art the resurrection and the life', etc. I cannot see this myself. The idea seems contradicted by Martha's subsequent conduct at the grave.

Musculus strongly maintains that Martha's confession, good as it was, was vague and imperfect. Lampe takes much the same view.

Thou art the Christ ... Son of God ... come ... world.

Here is Martha's statement of her belief. It contains three great points: (1) that Jesus was the Christ, the anointed One, the Messiah; (2) that he was the Son of God; (3) that he was the promised Redeemer, who was to come into the world. She goes no further, and probably she could not. Yet considering the time she lived in, the universal unbelief of the Jewish nation, and the wonderful difference in the views of believers before the crucifixion and after, I regard it as a noble and glorious confession, and even fuller than Peter's in Matthew 16:16. Melanchthon points out the great superiority of Martha's faith to that of the most intellectual heathen, in a long and interesting passage.

It is easy to say that Martha's faith was rather vague, and that she ought to have seen everything more clearly. But we at this period of time, and with all our advantages, are very poor judges of such a matter. Dark and dim as her views were, it was a great thing for a solitary Jewish woman to have got hold of so much truth, when, within two miles, in Jerusalem, all who held such a creed as hers were excommunicated and persecuted.

Let us note that people's views of truth may be very defective on some points, and yet they may have the root of the matter in them. Martha evidently did not yet fully realize that Christ was the resurrection and the life: but she had learned the alphabet of Christianity,—Christ's Messiahship and divinity, and doubtless learned more in time. We must not condemn people hastily or harshly, because they do not see all at once.

Chrysostom says, 'Martha seems to me not to understand Christ's saying. She was conscious it was some great thing, but did not perceive the whole meaning, so that when asked one thing she answered another.'

Toletus remarks, 'Martha thought she believed everything Christ said, while she believed him to be the true promised Messiah. And she did truly believe, but her faith was implicit and general. It is just as if some rustic, being questioned about some proposition of faith which he does not quite comprehend, replies, "I believe in the Holy Church." So here Martha said, "I believe, Lord, that thou art the true Christ, and that all things thou sayest are true"; and yet she did not distinctly perceive them.' This is a remarkable testimony from a Romanist.

Ought we not, perhaps, to make some allowance for the distress and affliction in which Martha was when she made her confession? Is it fair to expect a person in her position to speak as distinctly and precisely as one not in trouble?

28.—*And when she had so said, etc.*

The affection of Martha for her sister appears here. Once assured that her Master was come, and perhaps somewhat cheered by the few words he spoke, she hastens home to tell Mary that Jesus was come, and had called for her. We are not told expressly that Jesus had mentioned Mary, but we may suppose that he did, and had asked where she was.

The word 'secretly' may be applied to the word which follows, if we like, and it would then mean that 'Martha called Mary, saying secretly ...' This is probably the correct rendering.

The words rendered 'is come' would be more literally translated, 'is present: is actually here'.

The expression 'the Master' is probably the name by which our Lord was familiarly known by the family at Bethany. It is literally, 'the Teacher'.

Bullinger remarks that the word 'secretly' is purposely inserted, to show that the Jews who followed Mary had no idea that Jesus was come. Had they known it, he thinks, they would not have followed her, and so would not have seen the miracle.

Hall evidently thinks that Martha told Mary 'secretly', for fear of the unbelieving Jews who were among the comforters. He remarks, 'Christianity doth not bid us abate anything of our wariness and honest policy: yea, it requires us to have no less of the serpent than of the dove.'

29.—*As soon as she heard, etc.*

The two last words in this sentence are both in the present tense. It would be more literally rendered, 'She, when she heard, arises quickly and comes to him.' It is evident, I think, that the sudden movement of Mary was not caused by hearing that Jesus was come, but that Jesus called for her.

It is not unlikely, from the word 'arose', that Mary was lying or sitting prostrate on the ground, under the pressure of grief. We may also well suppose that our Lord, who doubtless knew her state, asked for her, in order to rouse her to exertion. When David heard that his child was dead, and nothing left for him to do but to be resigned, he 'arose from the earth' (2 Sam. 12:20).

CHAPTER FOUR

John 11:30-37

30 Now Jesus was not yet come into the town, but was in that place where Martha met him.

31 The Jews then which were with her in the house, and comforted her, when they saw Mary, that she rose up hastily and went out, followed her, saying, She goeth unto the grave to weep there.

32 Then when Mary was come where Jesus was, and saw him, she fell down at his feet, saying unto him, Lord, if thou hadst been here, my brother had not died.

33 When Jesus therefore saw her weeping, and the Jews also weeping which came with her, he groaned in the spirit, and was troubled,

34 And said, Where have ye laid him? They said unto him, Lord, come and see.

35 Jesus wept.

36 Then said the Jews, Behold how he loved him!

37 And some of them said, Could not this man, which opened the eyes of the blind, have caused that even this man should not have died?

NOT many passages in the New Testament are more wonderful than the simple narrative contained in these eight verses. It brings out, in a most beautiful light, the sympathizing character of our Lord Jesus Christ. It shows us him who is 'able … to save them to the uttermost that come unto God by him' (Heb. 7:25), as able to feel as he is to save. It shows us him who is one with the Father, and the Maker of all things, entering into human sorrows, and shedding human tears.

We learn, for one thing, in these verses, *how great a blessing God sometimes bestows on actions of kindness and sympathy.*

It seems that the house of Martha and Mary at Bethany was filled with mourners when Jesus arrived. Many of these mourners, no doubt, knew nothing of the inner life of these holy women. Their faith, their hope, their love to Christ, their discipleship, were things of which they were wholly ignorant. But they felt for them in their heavy bereavement, and kindly came to offer what comfort they could. By so doing they reaped a rich and unexpected reward. They beheld the greatest miracle that Jesus ever wrought. They were eye-witnesses when Lazarus came forth from the tomb. To many of them, we may well believe, that day was a spiritual birth. The raising of Lazarus led to a resurrection in their souls. How small sometimes are the hinges on which eternal life appears to depend! If these people had not sympathized they might never have been saved.

We need not doubt that these things were written for our learning. To show sympathy and kindness to the sorrowful is good for our own souls, whether we know it or not. To visit the fatherless and widows in their affliction, to weep with them that weep, to try to bear one another's burdens, and lighten one another's cares,—all this will make no atonement for sin, and will not take us to heaven. Yet it is healthy employment for our hearts, and employment which none ought to despise. Few perhaps are aware that one secret of being miserable is to live only for ourselves, and one secret of being happy is to try to make others happy, and to do a little good in the world. It is not for nothing that these words were written by Solomon, 'It is better to go to the house of mourning, than to go to the house of feasting':—'The heart of the wise is in the house of mourning; but the heart of fools is in the house of mirth' (Eccles. 7:2, 4). The saying of our Lord is too much overlooked: 'Whosoever shall give to drink unto one of these little ones a cup of cold water only in the name of a disciple, verily I say unto you, he shall in no wise lose his reward' (Matt. 10:42). The friends of Martha and Mary found that promise wonderfully verified. In an age of peculiar selfishness and self-indulgence, it would be well if they had more imitators.

We learn, for another thing, *what a depth of tender sympathy there is in Christ's heart towards his people*. We read that when our Lord saw Mary weeping, and the Jews also weeping with her, 'He groaned in the spirit and was troubled.' We read even more than this. He gave outward expression to his feelings: he 'wept'. He knew perfectly well that the sorrow of the family of Bethany would soon be turned into joy, and that Lazarus in a few minutes would be restored to his sisters. But though he knew all this, he 'wept'.

This weeping of Christ is deeply instructive. It shows us that it is not sinful to sorrow. Weeping and mourning are sadly trying to flesh and blood, and make us feel the weakness of our mortal nature. But they are not in themselves wrong. Even the Son of God wept.—It shows us that deep feeling is not a thing of which we need be ashamed. To be cold and stoical and unmoved in the sight of sorrow is no sign of grace. There is nothing unworthy of a child of God in tears. Even the Son of God could weep.—It shows us, above all, that the Saviour in whom believers trust is a most tender and feeling Saviour. He is one who can be touched with sympathy for our infirmities. When we turn to him in the hour of trouble, and pour out our hearts before him, he knows what we go through, and can pity. And he is One who never changes. Though he now sits at God's right hand in heaven, his heart is still the same that it was upon earth. We have an Advocate with the Father, who, when he was upon earth, could weep.

Let us remember these things in daily life, and never be ashamed of walking in our Master's footsteps. Let us strive to be men and women of a tender heart and a sympathizing spirit. Let us never be ashamed to weep with them that weep, and rejoice with them that rejoice. Well would it be for the church and the world if there were more Christians of this stamp and character! The church would be far more beautiful, and the world would be far more happy.

NOTES ON JOHN 11:30-37

30.—Now Jesus was not yet come, etc.

The Greek word for 'come' is in the preterperfect tense. The sentence, translated literally, would be, 'Jesus had not yet come into the town' when Martha left him to tell Mary, but was still waiting or remaining in the place outside Bethany, where Martha at first met him. The word 'town' would be more correctly rendered 'village', according to our present acceptation of the word. Yet it is fair to remember that words change their meaning with lapse of time. Even at this day a little Suffolk village of 1,400 people is called a 'town' by many of its inhabitants.

Calvin thinks that Jesus remained outside Bethany by Martha's request, that his life might not be endangered.

31.—The Jews then ... comforted her ... saw Mary ... followed her.

It is probable that the persons here mentioned formed a considerable number,—as many as could crowd into the house. 'Comforted' in the Greek is the present participle, and implies that they were actually employed in comforting Mary. Concerning the manner of comforting on such occasions, we know nothing certain. People who only talk commonplaces are miserable comforters, and far worse than Job's friends, who sat for seven days saying nothing at all. It may be that among the Jews the mere presence of courteous and sympathizing people was thought a kind attention, and soothed the feelings of the bereaved. The customs of nations differ widely in such matters.

It is evident these Jews did not hear Martha's message, and knew nothing of Jesus being near. Some of them perhaps, had they known it, would not have followed Mary; not knowing, they all followed without exception, and unexpectedly became eye-witnesses of a stupendous miracle. All they knew was that Mary went out hastily. They followed in a spirit of kind sympathy, and by so doing reaped a great blessing.

Rupertus shrewdly remarks that the Jews did not follow Martha, when she ran to meet Jesus, but did follow Mary. He conjectures that Mary's affliction was deeper and more overwhelming than Martha's, and her friends devoted themselves more to comfort her, as needing most consolation. Yet the simpler reason seems to be that when *both* sisters had left the house, the friends could hardly do anything else but go out and follow.

She goeth ... grave to weep there.

We must suppose from this sentence, that weeping at the grave of dead friends was a custom among the Jews in our Lord's time. In estimating such a custom, which to most thinking persons may seem as useless as rubbing a wound, and very likely to keep up pain without healing, it is only fair to remember that Old Testament views of the state after death were not nearly so well lighted and comfortable as ours. The removal of death's sting, the resurrection and paradise, were things not nearly so well understood even by the best saints before Christ, as they were after Christ rose again. To most of the Jews in our Lord's time, we can well believe that death was regarded as the end of all happiness and comfort, and the state after death as a dreary blank. When Sadducees, who said there was 'no resurrection', were chief rulers and high priests, we may well suppose that the sorrow of many Jews over the death of friends, was a 'sorrow without hope'. Even at this day, 'the place of wailing' at Jerusalem, where the Jews assemble to weep over the foundation stones of the old temple, is a proof that their habit of weeping over crushed hopes is not yet extinct.

32.—*Then when Mary, etc.*

We see in this verse that as soon as Mary met our Lord, the first thing she said was almost exactly what Martha had said in the twenty-first verse, and the remarks made there need not be repeated. The similarity shows, at any rate, that throughout the illness of Lazarus, the thoughts of the two sisters had been running in one and the same direction. Both had built all their hopes on Jesus coming. Both had felt confidence that his coming would have saved their brother's life. Both were bitterly disappointed that he did not come. Both had probably kept saying the same words repeatedly, 'If our Master would only come, Lazarus would not die.' There are, however, one or two touches of difference between the two sisters, here as elsewhere. Let us note them.

Mary 'fell down' at our Lord's feet, and Martha did not. She was made of softer, feebler character than Martha, and was more completely crushed and overcome than her sister.

Mary fell down at our Lord's feet when she 'saw' him. Up to that moment probably she had borne up, and had run to the place where Martha told her Jesus was waiting. But when she actually saw her Master, and remembered how she had longed for a sight of him for some days, her feelings overcame her, and she broke down. The eyes have a great effect on the feelings of the heart. People often bear up pretty well, till they *see* something that calls up thoughts.

I do not perceive any ground for thinking, as Calvin does, that this 'falling at our Lord's feet' was an act of worship, a recognition of our Lord's divinity. It is much more natural and reasonable to regard it as the mere expression of Mary's state of feeling.

Trapp remarks that the words of Mary in this verse and of Martha in the former one, show that we are all naturally disposed to make too much of Christ's bodily presence.

33.—*When Jesus therefore saw her, etc.*

This is one of those verses which bring out very strongly the real humanity of our Lord, and his power to sympathize with his people. As a real man, he was specially moved when he saw Mary and the Jews weeping. As God, he had no need to hear their plaintive language, and to see their tears in order to learn that they were afflicted. He knew perfectly all their feelings. Yet as man he was like ourselves, peculiarly stirred by the *sight* of sorrow: for human nature is so constituted, that grief is eminently contagious. If one in a company is deeply touched, and begins to weep, it is extremely likely that others will weep also. This power of sympathy our Lord evidently had in full possession. He *saw* weeping, and he wept.

Let us carefully remark that our Lord never changes. He did not leave behind him his human nature when he ascended up into heaven. At this moment, at God's right hand, he can be touched with the feeling of our infirmities, and can understand tears as well as ever. Our great High Priest is the very Friend that our souls need, able to save as God, able to feel as man. To talk of the Virgin Mary feeling for sinners more than Jesus, is to say that which is ignorant and blasphemous. To teach that we can need any other priest, when Jesus is such a feeling Saviour, is to teach what is senseless and absurd.

He groaned in the spirit.

There is considerable difficulty about this expression. The word rendered 'groaned' is only used five times in the New Testament. In Matthew 9:30, and Mark 1:43, it is 'straitly charged'. In Mark 14:5, it is 'murmured'. Here, and at verse 38 below, it is 'groaned'. Now what is precisely meant by the phrase?

(*a*) Some, as Œcolampadius, Brentius, Chemnitius, Flacius, and Ferus, maintain firmly that the notion of anger, indignation, and stern rebuke, is inseparable from the word 'groaned'. They think that the latent idea is the deep and holy indignation with which our Lord was moved at the sight of the ravages which death had made, and the misery sin and the devil had brought into the world. They say it implies the stern and righteous wrath with which the deliverer of a country tyrannized over and trampled down by a rebel, regards the desolation and destruction which the rebel has caused.

(*b*) Some add to this view the idea that 'in the spirit' means that our Lord groaned through the Holy Ghost, or by the divine Spirit which dwelt in him without measure, or by the power of his Godhead.

(*c*) Some, as Chrysostom, Theophylact, and Euthymius, think 'groaned in the spirit' means that Christ rebuked his own natural feelings by his divine nature, or restrained his trouble, and in so doing was greatly disturbed.

(*d*) Some, as Gomarus and Lampe, consider that our Lord was moved to holy sorrow and indignation at the sight of the unbelief even of Martha and Mary (expressed by their immoderate grief, as if the case of Lazarus was hopeless), as well as at the sight of the unbelief of the Jews.

(*e*) Some, as Bullinger, Gualter, Diodati, Grotius, Maldonatus, Jansenius, Rollock, and Hutcheson, consider that the phrase simply expresses the highest and deepest kind of inward agitation of mind, an agitation in which grief, compassion, and holy detestation of sin's work in the world, were all mingled and combined. This agitation, however, was entirely inward at present; it was not bodily, but spiritual; not in the flesh, but in the spirit. As Burgon says, the 'spirit' here means Christ's *inward* soul. I prefer this opinion to the former one, though I fully admit it has difficulties. But it is allowed by Schleusner and Parkhurst, and seems the view of Tyndall, Cranmer, and the Geneva version, as well as of our own.

And was troubled.

This expression is to my mind even more difficult than the one which immediately precedes it. It would be literally translated, as our marginal reading has it, 'He troubled himself.' In fact, Wycliffe translates it so. Now what can this mean?

Some maintain that in our Lord's mysterious person the human nature was so entirely subordinated to the divine, that the human passions and affections never moved unless influenced and actuated by the divine nature, and that here to show his sympathy, he 'troubled himself'. Thus Rupertus remarks that 'if he had not troubled himself, no one else could have troubled him'. I confess that I regard this view with a little suspicion. It seems to me to imply that our Lord's human nature was not like ours, and that his humanity was like an instrument played upon by his divinity, but in itself dead and passive until its music was called out. To my mind there is something dangerous in this.

I prefer to think that our Lord as man had all the feelings, passions, and affections of a man, but all under such perfect control that they never exceeded as ours do, and were never even very demonstrative, excepting on great occasions. As Beza says, there was no 'disorder' in his emotions. Here I think he saw an occasion for exhibiting a very deep degree of sorrow and sympathy, partly from the sorrowful sight he beheld, and partly from his love to Mary, Martha, and Lazarus. Therefore he greatly disturbed and 'troubled himself'.

It still admits of a question whether the phrase may not be simply a Hebraism for 'He was troubled' (compare 1 Sam. 30:6, and 2 Sam. 12:18). Hammond says it is a Hebrew idiom.

When all has been said, we must not forget that the phrase touches a very delicate and mysterious subject: that subject is the precise nature of the union of two natures in our Lord's person. That he was at the same time perfect God and perfect man, is an article of the Christian faith; but how far the divine nature acted on the human, and to what extent it checked and influenced the action of human passions and feelings, are very deep points, which we have no line completely to fathom. After all, not the least part of our difficulty is that we can form no clear and adequate conception of a human nature entirely without sin.

One thing, at any rate, is abundantly clear from this passage: there is nothing wrong or wicked in being greatly moved by the sight of sorrow, so long as we keep our feelings under control. To be always cold, unfeeling, and unsympathizing, may appear to some very dignified and philosophical. But though it may suit a Stoic, it is not consistent with the character of a Christian. Sympathy is not sinful, but Christlike.

Theophylact observes that Christ 'teaches us by his own example the due measure of joy and grief. The absence altogether of sympathy and sorrow is brutal: the excess of them is womanly.'

Melanchthon observes that none of Christ's miracles seem to have been done without some great mental emotion (Luke 8:46). He supposes that here at this verse, there was a great conflict with Satan in our Lord's mind, and that he wrestled in prayer for the raising of Lazarus, and then thanked God afterwards that the prayer was heard. Calvin takes much the same view.

Œcolampadius observes that we must not think Christ had a human body only, and not a human soul. He had a soul like our own in all things, sin only excepted, and capable of all our feelings and emotions.

Piscator and Trapp compare the trouble of spirit which our Lord went through, to the disturbance and agitation of perfectly clear water in a perfectly clear glass vessel. However great the agitation, the water remains clear.

Musculus reverently remarks that after all there is something about this 'groaning in spirit and troubling himself', which cannot be fully explained.

34.—And said, Where have ye laid him?

We cannot suppose that our Lord, who knew all things, even to the moment of Lazarus' death, could really need to be informed where Lazarus was buried. He asks what he does here partly as a kind friend to show his deep sympathy and interest in the grave of his friend, and partly to give further proof that there was no collusion in the matter of Lazarus' burial, and that he had nothing to do with the choice of his tomb, in order to concert an imposture about raising him. In short, those who heard him publicly ask this question, would see that this was no pre-arranged and pre-contrived miracle.

Quesnel remarks, 'Christ does not ask out of ignorance, any more than God did when he said, "Adam, where art thou?"'

They said … Lord, come and see.

Who they were that said this, we do not exactly know. It was probably the common saying of all the party of mourners who stood around while Jesus talked with Mary. They did not know why our Lord wished to see the grave. They may possibly have supposed that he wished to accompany Mary and Martha, and to weep at the grave. At any rate the question and answer secured a large attendance of companions, as the disciples and our Lord went to the place where Lazarus was buried.

35.—Jesus wept.

This wonderful little verse has given rise to an enormous amount of comment. The difficulty is to select thoughts, and not to overload the subject.

The Greek word rendered 'wept' is not the same as that used for 'weeping' in verse 33, but totally different. There the weeping is a weeping accompanied by demonstrative lamentation. Here the word would be more literally and accurately rendered 'shed tears'. In fact it is the only place in the New Testament where this word for 'weep' is used.

There are three occasions where our Lord is recorded to have wept, in the Gospels: once when he beheld the city (Luke 19:41), once in the garden of Gethsemane (Matt. 26:39, and Heb. 5:7), and here. We never read of his laughing, and only once of his rejoicing (Luke 10:21).

The reasons assigned by commentators why our Lord wept here, before he raised Lazarus, are various and curious.

(*a*) Some think that he wept to see the ravages made by death and sin.

(*b*) Some, as Hilary, think that he wept to think of the unbelief of the Jews.

(*c*) Some think that he wept to see how weak and feeble was the faith of Mary and Martha.

(*d*) Some, as Jerome and Ferus, think that he wept at the thought of the sorrow Lazarus would go through by returning to a sinful world.

(*e*) Some think that he wept out of sympathy with the affliction of his friends at Bethany, in order to give an eternal proof to his church that he can feel with us and for us.

I believe this last opinion is the true one.

We learn the great practical lesson from this verse, that there is nothing unworthy of a Christian in tears. There is nothing unmanly, dishonourable, unwise, or feeble, in being full of sympathy with the afflicted, and ready to weep with them that weep. Indeed, it is curious to gather up the many instances we have in Scripture of great men weeping.

We may draw great comfort from the thought that the Saviour in whom we are bid to trust is one who can weep, and is as able to feel as he is able to save.

We may learn the reality of our Lord's humanity very strongly from this little verse. He was one who could hunger, thirst, sleep, eat, drink, speak, walk, groan, be wearied, wonder, feel indignant, rejoice, like any of ourselves, and yet without sin; and above all, he could weep. I read that there is 'joy in the presence of the angels of God' (Luke 15:10), but I never read of angels weeping. Tears are peculiar to flesh and blood.

Chrysostom remarks that 'John, who enters into higher statements about our Lord's nature than any of the Evangelists, also descends lower than any in describing his bodily affections.'

36.—*Then said the Jews, Behold ... loved him!*

This sentence is the expression partly of surprise, which comes out in the word 'behold'; and partly of admiration,— what a loving and tender-hearted Teacher this is! It gives the idea that those who said this were the few unprejudiced Jews who had come to Bethany to comfort Mary and Martha, and afterward believed when they saw Lazarus raised.

Let us observe that of all graces, love is the one which most arrests the attention and influences the opinion of the world.

37.—*And some of them said, etc.*

This sentence sounds to me like the language of enemies determined to believe nothing good of our Lord, and prepared to pick a hole or find a fault if possible, in anything that he did. Does not a sarcastic sneer ring throughout it? 'Could not this man, if he really did open the eyes of that blind person at Jerusalem last autumn, have prevented this friend of his from dying? If he really is the Messiah and the Christ, and really does work such wonderful works, why has he not prevented all this sorrow? If he really loved Lazarus and his sisters, why did he not prove his love by keeping him back from the grave? Is it not plain that he is not almighty? He cannot do everything. He could open the eyes of a blind man, but he could not prevent death carrying off his friend. If he was able to prevent Lazarus dying, why did he not do it? If he was not able, it is clear there are some things he cannot do.'

We should note that 'the blind' is a word in the singular number. It is evidently the blind man at Jerusalem whose case is referred to.

Let us note that nothing will convince, or satisfy, or silence some wicked men. Even when Christ is before them, they are cavilling, and doubting, and finding fault. What right have Christ's ministers to be surprised if they meet with the same treatment?

Musculus remarks on the satanic malice which this sentence displays. It is the old sceptical spirit of cavilling and questioning. Unbelief is always saying 'Why? and why? and why?' 'If this man was such a friend of Lazarus, and loved him so much, why did he let him die?'

CHAPTER FIVE

John 11:38-46

38 Jesus therefore again groaning in himself cometh to the grave. It was a cave, and a stone lay upon it.

39 Jesus said, Take ye away the stone. Martha, the sister of him that was dead, saith unto him, Lord, by this time he stinketh: for he hath been dead four days.

40 Jesus saith unto her, Said I not unto thee, that, if thou wouldest believe, thou shouldest see the glory of God?

41 Then they took away the stone from the place where the dead was laid. And Jesus lifted up his eyes, and said, Father, I thank thee that thou hast heard me.

42 And I knew that thou hearest me always: but because of the people which stand by I said it, that they may believe that thou hast sent me.

43 And when he thus had spoken, he cried with a loud voice, Lazarus, come forth.

44 And he that was dead came forth, bound hand and foot with graveclothes: and his face was bound about with a napkin. Jesus saith unto them, Loose him, and let him go.

45 Then many of the Jews which came to Mary, and had seen the things which Jesus did, believed on him.

46 But some of them went their ways to the Pharisees, and told them what things Jesus had done.

THESE verses record one of the greatest miracles the Lord Jesus Christ ever worked, and supply an unanswerable proof of his divinity. He whose voice could bring back from the grave one that had been four days dead, must indeed have been very God! The miracle itself is described in such simple language that no human comment can throw light upon it. But the sayings of our Lord on this occasion are peculiarly interesting, and demand special notice.

We should mark, first, *our Lord's words about the stone which lay upon the grave of Lazarus.* We read that he said to those around him, when he came to the place of burial, 'Take ye away the stone.'

Now why did our Lord say this? It was doubtless as easy for him to command the stone to roll away untouched, as to call a dead body from the tomb. But such was not his mode of proceeding. Here, as in other cases, he chose to give man something to do. Here, as elsewhere, he taught the great lesson that his almighty power was not meant to destroy man's responsibility. Even when he was ready and willing to raise the dead, he would not have man stand by altogether idle.

Let us treasure up this in our memories. It involves a point of great importance. In doing spiritual good to others,—in training up our children for heaven,—in following after holiness in our own daily walk,—in all these things it is undoubtedly true that we are weak and helpless. 'Without [Christ we] can do nothing' (John 15:5). But still we must remember that Christ expects us to do what we can. 'Take ye away the stone' is the daily command which he gives us. Let us beware that we do not stand still in idleness, under the pretence of humility. Let us daily try to do what we can, and in the trying, Christ will meet us and grant his blessing.

We should mark, secondly, *the words which our Lord addressed to Martha, when she objected to the stone being removed from the grave.* The faith of this holy woman completely broke down, when the cave where her beloved brother lay was about to be thrown open. She could not believe that it was of any use. 'Lord', she cries, 'by this time he stinketh.' And then comes in the solemn reproof of our Lord: 'Said I not unto thee, that, if thou wouldest believe, thou shouldest see the glory of God?'

That sentence is rich in meaning. It is far from unlikely that it contains a reference to the message which had been sent to Martha and Mary, when their brother first fell sick. It may be meant to remind Martha that her Master had sent her word, 'This sickness is not unto death, but for the glory of God.' But it is perhaps more likely that our Lord desired to recall to Martha's mind the old lesson he had taught her all through his ministry, the duty of always believing. It is as though he said, 'Martha, Martha, thou art forgetting the great doctrine of faith, which I have ever taught thee. Believe, and all will be well. Fear not: only believe.'

The lesson is one which we can never know too well. How apt our faith is to break down in time of trial! How easy it is to talk of faith in the days of health and prosperity, and how hard to practise it in the days of darkness, when neither sun, moon, nor stars appear! Let us lay to heart what our Lord says in this place. Let us pray for such stores of inward faith, that when our turn comes to suffer, we may suffer patiently and believe all is well. The Christian who has ceased to say, 'I must see, and then I will believe', and has learned to say, 'I believe, and by and by I shall see', has reached a high degree in the school of Christ.

We should mark, thirdly, *the words which our Lord addressed to God the Father, when the stone was taken from the grave.* We read that he said, 'Father, I thank thee that thou hast heard me. And I knew that thou hearest me always: but because of the people which stand by I said it, that they may believe that thou hast sent me.'

This wonderful language is totally unlike anything said by prophets or apostles, when they worked miracles. In fact, it is not prayer, but praise. It evidently implies a constant mysterious communion going on between Jesus and his Father in heaven, which it is past the power of man either to explain or conceive. We need not doubt that here, as elsewhere in St John, our Lord meant to teach the Jews the entire and complete unity there was between him and his Father, in all that he did, as well as in all that he taught. Once more he would remind them that he did not come among them as a mere prophet, but as the Messiah, who was sent by the Father, and who was one with the Father.

Once more he would have them know that as the words which he spake were the very words which the Father gave him to speak, so the works which he wrought were the very works which the Father gave him to do. In short, he was the promised Messiah, whom the Father always hears, because he and the Father are one.

Deep and high as this truth is, it is for the peace of our souls to believe it thoroughly, and to grasp it tightly. Let it be a settled principle of our religion, that the Saviour in whom we trust is nothing less than eternal God, One whom the Father hears always, One who in very deed is God's Fellow. A clear view of the dignity of our Mediator's person is one secret of inward comfort. Happy is he who can say, 'I know whom I have believed, and am persuaded that he is able to keep that which I have committed unto him' (2 Tim. 1:12).

We should mark, lastly, *the words which our Lord addressed to Lazarus when he raised him from the grave.* We read that 'He cried with a loud voice, Lazarus, come forth.' At the sound of that voice, the king of terrors at once yielded up his lawful captive, and the insatiable grave gave up its prey. At once, 'He that was dead came forth, bound hand and foot with graveclothes.'

The greatness of this miracle cannot possibly be exaggerated. The mind of man can scarcely take in the vastness of the work that was done. Here, in open day, and before many hostile witnesses, a man, four days dead, was restored to life in a moment. Here was public proof that our Lord had absolute power over the material world! A corpse already corrupt, was made alive!—Here was public proof that our Lord had absolute power over the world of spirits! A soul that had left its earthly tenement was called back from paradise, and joined once more to its owner's body. Well may the church of Christ maintain that he who could work such works was 'over all, God blessed for ever' (Rom. 9:5).

Let us turn from the whole passage with thoughts of comfort and consolation. Comfortable is the thought that the loving Saviour of sinners, on whose mercy our souls entirely depend, is one who has all power in heaven and earth, and is mighty to save.—Comfortable is the thought that there is no sinner too far gone in sin for Christ to raise and convert. He that stood by the grave of Lazarus can say to the vilest of men, 'Come forth: loose him, and let him go.'—Comfortable, not least, is the thought that when we ourselves lie down in the grave, we may lie down in the full assurance that we shall rise again. The voice that called Lazarus forth will one day pierce our tombs, and bid soul and body come together. 'The trumpet shall sound, and the dead shall be raised incorruptible, and we shall be changed' (1 Cor. 15:52).

Notes on John 11:38-46

38.—Jesus ... groaning ... cometh ... grave.

The word here rendered 'groaning' is the same that was used at verse 33, and the same remarks apply to it. The only difference is that here it is 'groaning in himself', and there 'groaning in the spirit'. This, however, confirms my impression that in the former verse 'in the spirit' simply means 'inwardly and spiritually', and that the general idea is 'under the influence of very strong inward emotion'.

The situation of the grave, we need not doubt, was outside the village of Bethany. There was no such thing as interment within a town allowed among the Jews, or indeed among ancient nations generally. The practice of burying the dead among the living is a barbarous modern innovation, reflecting little credit on Christians.

Calvin remarks, 'Christ approaches the sepulchre as a champion preparing for a contest; and we need not wonder that he groans, as the violent tyranny of death, which he had to conquer, is placed before his eyes.'

Œcolampadius and Musculus think that the unbelieving, sneering remark of the Jews in the preceding verse, is the reason why our Lord 'again groaned'. Bullinger thinks that the renewed emotion of our Lord was simply occasioned by the sight of the grave.

It was a cave, and a stone lay upon it.

Graves among the Jews seem to have been of three kinds. (1) Sometimes, but rarely, they were holes dug down into the ground, like our own (see Luke 11:44). (2) Most frequently they were caves hewn horizontally into the side of a rock, with a stone placed against the mouth. This was most probably the kind of new tomb in which our Lord was laid. (3) Sometimes they were caves in which there was a sloping, downward descent. This appears to have been the description of the grave in which Lazarus was buried. It says distinctly that 'a stone lay *upon* it'.

No doubt these particulars are specified to supply incidental proof of the reality of Lazarus' death and burial.

39.—*Jesus said, Take ye away the stone.*

The expression here conveys the idea of 'lifting up' to take away. It is the same word that is rendered 'lifted up' in verse 41.

The use of this word greatly strengthens the idea that the grave was a descending cave, and not a horizontal one. When our Lord rose again, the stone was 'rolled back from the door', and not lifted up (Matt. 28:2).

By calling on the crowd of attendants to take away the stone, our Lord effected two things. Firstly, he impressed on the minds of all engaged the reality and truth of the miracle he was about to perform. Everyone who lent a hand to lift the huge stone and remove it, would remember it, and become a witness. He would be able to say, 'I myself helped to lift up the stone. I myself am sure there was no imposture. There was a dead body inside the grave.' In fact, we cannot doubt that the smell rising from the bottom of the cave would tell anyone who helped to lift the stone what there was there.— Secondly, our Lord teaches us the simple lesson that he would have man do what he can. Man cannot raise the soul, and give life, but he can often remove the stone.

Flacius points out the likeness between this command and the command at Cana to fill the waterpots with water (John 2:7).

That the stones placed at the mouth of graves in Palestine were very large, and not easily moved, we may see from Mark 16:3.

Martha, the sister of him, etc.

This is a remarkable sentence, and teaches several important things.

(*a*) It certifies, for the last time, the reality of Lazarus' death. He was not in a swoon or a trance. His own sister, who had doubtless seen him die, and closed his eyes, declares before the crowd of lookers-on, that Lazarus had been dead four days, and was fast going to corruption. This we may well believe in such a climate as that of Palestine.

(*b*) It proves, beyond a reasonable doubt, that there was no imposture, no collusion, no concerted deception, arranged between the family of Bethany and our Lord. Here is the sister of Lazarus actually questioning the propriety of our Lord's order, and publicly saying in effect that it is no use to move the stone, that nothing can now be done to deliver her brother from the power of death. Like the eleven apostles, after Jesus himself rose, Martha was not a willing and prepared witness, but a resisting and unwilling one.

(*c*) It teaches, not least, how much unbelief there is in a believer's heart at the bottom. Here is holy Martha, with all her faith in our Lord's Messiahship, shrinking and breaking down at this most critical point. She cannot believe that there is any use in removing the stone. She suggests, impulsively and anxiously, her doubt whether our Lord remembers how long her brother has been dead.

It is not for nothing that we are specially told it was 'Martha, the sister of him that was dead', who said this. If even she could say this, and raise objections, the idea of imposture and deception becomes absurd.

Some writers object to putting the full literal meaning on the Greek word rendered 'stinketh': but I can see nothing in the objection. We need not suppose that the body of Lazarus was different to other bodies. Moreover, it was just as easy to our Lord to raise a corpse four days dead, as one only four hours dead. In either case, the grand difficulty to be overcome would be the same: viz., to change death into life. Indeed it is worth considering whether this fact about Lazarus is not specially mentioned in order to show our Lord's power to restore man's corrupt and decayed body at the last day, and to make it a glorious body.

Let us note here what a humbling lesson death teaches. So terrible and painful is the corruption of a body, when the breath leaves it, that even those who love us most are glad to bury us out of sight (Gen. 23:4).

Musculus suggests that Martha had so little idea what our Lord was going to do, that she supposed he only wanted to see Lazarus' face once more. This is perhaps going too far.

The Greek for 'dead four days' is a singular expression, and one that cannot be literally rendered in English. It would be 'He is a person of four days'; and it may possibly mean, 'He has been buried four days.' Raphelius gives examples from Herodotus and Xenophon, which makes it possible that it means either dead or buried.

Lightfoot mentions a very curious tradition of the Jews: 'They say after death the spirit hovers about the sepulchre, waiting to see if it may return to the body. But when it sees the look of the face of the corpse changed, then it hovers no more, but leaves the body to itself.' He also adds, 'They do not certify of the dead, except within three days after decease; for after three days the countenance changes.'

40.—*Jesus saith … Said I not, etc.*

This gentle but firm reproof is remarkable. It is not clear to what our Lord refers in the words, 'Said I not.'

(*a*) Some think, as Rupertus, that he refers to the message he sent at the beginning: 'This sickness is not unto death, but for the glory of God.'

(*b*) Some think that he refers to the conversation he had with Martha when she first met him outside Bethany.

(*c*) Some think that he refers to words he had often used in discoursing with Martha and Mary, on former occasions.

The point is one which must be left open, as we have no means of settling it. My own impression is that there is probably a reference to the message which our Lord sent back to the sisters at first, when Lazarus was sick. I fancy there must have been something more said at that time which is not recorded, and that our Lord reminded Martha of this. At the same time I cannot doubt that our Lord constantly taught the family of Bethany, and all his disciples, that believing is the grand secret of seeing God's glorious works.—'If thou canst believe, all things are possible to him that believeth.' 'He did not many mighty works there because of their unbelief' (Mark 9:23; Matt. 13:58). Unbelief, in a certain sense, seems to tie the hands and limit the power of omnipotence.

Let us note that if we would see much we must first believe. Man's natural idea is just the reverse: he would first see, and then believe.

Let us note that even the best believers need reminding of Christ's sayings, and are apt to forget them. 'Said I not unto thee.' It is a little sentence we should often call to mind.

41.—Then they took away the stone ... laid.

Martha's interruption seems to me to have caused a little pause in the proceedings. She being the nearest relative of Lazarus, and having probably arranged everything concerning his burial, and provided his tomb, we may well believe that her speech made the bystanders hesitate to move the stone. When, however, they heard our Lord's solemn reply, and observed that she was silenced, and made no further objection, 'then' they proceeded to do what our Lord desired.

Hall remarks, 'They that laid their hands to the stone doubtless held still awhile, when Martha spoke, and looked one while on Christ, another while on Martha, to hear what issue of resolution would follow so important an objection.'

And Jesus lifted up his eyes, and said.

We now reach a point of thrilling and breathless interest. The stone had been removed from the mouth of the cave. Our Lord stands before the open grave, and the crowd stands around, awaiting anxiously to see what would happen next. Nothing appears from the tomb. There is no sign of life at present: but while all are eagerly looking and listening, our Lord addresses his Father in heaven in a most solemn manner, lifting up his eyes, and speaking audibly to him in the hearing of all the crowd. The reason he explains in the next verse. Now, for the last time, about to work his mightiest miracle, he once more makes a public declaration that he did nothing separate from his Father in heaven, and that in this and all his works there is a mysterious and intimate union between himself and the Father.

We should note how he suits the action to the word. 'He lifted up his eyes' (compare John 17:1). He showed that he was addressing an unseen Father in heaven.

Father, I thank thee that thou hast heard me.

This is a remarkable expression. Our Lord begins with 'thanks', when man would have expected him to offer prayer. How shall we explain it?

(*a*) Some think that our Lord refers to prayer he had put up to the Father concerning the death of Lazarus, from the moment that he heard of his illness, and to his present firm conviction that those prayers had been heard, and were going to receive a public answer.

(*b*) Others think that there is no reason to suppose that our Lord refers to any former or remote prayer; that there was a constant, hourly, minutely communication between himself and his heavenly Father; and that to pray, and return thanks for the answer to prayer, were actions which in his experience were very closely connected.

The subject is a deep and mysterious one, and I shrink from giving a very positive opinion about it. That our Lord constantly prayed on all occasions, we know from the Gospels. That he prayed sometimes with great agony of mind and with tears, we also know (Heb. 5:7). But how far he could know anything of that peculiar struggle which we poor sinners have to carry on with doubt, fear, and anxiety, in our prayers, is another question altogether, and very hard to answer. One might suppose that One who was as man, entirely holy, humble, and without sin, might be able to thank for prayer heard, almost as soon as prayer was offered. Upon this theory the sentence before us would be plain: 'I pray that Lazarus may be raised; and I thank thee at the same time for hearing my prayer, as I know thou dost.'

And yet we must not forget two of our Lord's prayers not granted, apparently: 'Father, save me from this hour';—

'Father ... let this cup pass from me' (John 12:27; Matt. 26:39). It is however only fair to say that the first of these prayers is greatly qualified by the context, and the second by the words, 'If it be possible.'

We may note here as elsewhere, what an example of thankfulness, as well as prayerfulness, our Lord always supplies. Well if it was followed! His people are always more ready to ask than to thank. The more grace in a heart the more humility, and the more humility the more praise.

Chrysostom remarks, 'Who now ever prayed in this manner? Before uttering any prayer, he saith, "I thank thee"; showing that he needed not prayer.' He also says that the real cause of our Lord saying this was to show the Jews he was no enemy of God, but did all his works according to his will.

Origen observes, 'If to those who pray worthily is given the promise in Isaiah, "Thou shalt cry, and he shall say, Here I am," what answer think we could our Lord receive? He was about to pray for the resurrection of Lazarus. He was heard by the Father before he prayed; his request was granted before it was made; and, therefore, he begins with thanks.'

Musculus, Flacius, and Glassius, think that our Lord refers to prayer he had been putting up secretly when he was 'groaning in spirit and troubled', and that he was then wrestling and agonizing in prayer, though those around him knew it not. We may remember that at the Red Sea we are not told of any audible prayer Moses offered, and yet the Lord says, 'Wherefore criest thou unto me?' (Exod. 14:15).

Quesnel observes, 'Christ being about to conclude his public life and preaching by the last and most illustrious of his miracles, returns solemn thanks to his Father for the power given to his human nature to prove the authority of his mission by miracles.'

Hall observes, 'Words express our hearts to men, thoughts to God. Well didst thou know, Lord, out of the self-sameness of thy will with the Father's, that if thou didst but think in thy heart that Lazarus should rise, he was now raised. It was not for thee to pray vocally and audibly, lest those captious hearers should say, thou didst all by entreaty, and nothing by power.'

42.—*And I knew that thou hearest, etc.*

This verse is so elliptical that the meaning can hardly be seen without a paraphrase. 'I do not give thee these thanks as if I had ever doubted thy willingness to hear me; on the contrary, I know well that thou always hearest me.—Thou dost not only hear all my prayers as man, both for myself and my people; thou dost also ever hear me, even as I hear thee, from the mystical union there is between the Father and the Son.—But I have now said this publicly, for the benefit of this crowd of people standing by the grave, in order that they may see and believe for the last time that I do no miracle without thee, and that I am the Messiah whom thou hast sent into the world. I would have them publicly hear me declare that I work this last great work as thy Sent One, and as a last evidence that I am the Christ.'

I cannot but think that there is a deep meaning about the expression, 'thou hearest me always' (compare John 5:30). But I admit the difficulty of the phrase, and would speak with diffidence.

It is impossible to imagine a more thorough open challenge to the attention of the Jews, than the language which preceded the raising of Lazarus. Before doing this stupendous work, our Lord proclaims that he is doing and speaking as he does, to supply a proof that the Father sent and commissioned him as the Christ. Was he the 'Sent One' or not? This, we must always remember, was the great question, of which he undertook to give proof. The Jews, moreover, said that he did his miracles by Beelzebub: let them hear that he did all by the power of God.

Bullinger remarks that our Lord seems to say, 'The Jews do not all understand that union and communion between me and thee, by which we are of the same will, power, and substance. Some of them even think that I work by the power of the devil. Therefore that all may believe that I come from thee, am sent by thee, am thy Son, equal to thee, light of light, very God of very God, I use expressions of this sort.'

Poole remarks, 'There is a great difference between God's hearing of Christ and hearing us. Christ and his Father have one essence, one nature, and one will.'

The following miracles were wrought by Christ without audible prayer, and with only an authoritative word Matthew 8:3; 9:6, 7; Mark 5:41, 42; 9:25-27; Luke 7:14, 15.

Wordsworth observes, 'Christ prayed to show that he was not against God, nor God against him, and that what he did was done with God's approval.'

43.—And when ... cried ... come forth.

In this verse we have the last and crowning stage of the miracle. Attention was concentrated on the grave and our Lord. The crowd looked on with breathless expectation; and then, while they looked, having secured their attention, our Lord bids Lazarus come forth out of the grave. The Greek

word for 'he cried' is only in this place applied to any voice
or utterance of our Lord. In Matthew 12:19, it is used, where
it is said of our Lord, 'He shall *not ... cry.*' Here it is evident
that he purposely used a very loud and piercing cry, that all
around might hear and take notice.

Theophylact thinks that Jesus 'cried aloud to contradict
the Gentile fable that the soul remained in the tomb with the
body. Therefore the soul of Lazarus is called to as if it were
absent, and a loud voice were necessary to summon it back.'
Euthymius suggests the same reason. This however seems an
odd idea.

On the other hand, Brentius, Grotius, and Lampe,
suggest that Jesus 'cried with a loud voice', to prevent the
Jews from saying that he muttered or whispered some magical
form, or words of enchantment, as witches did.

Ferus observes that our Lord did not say, 'In the name of
my Father, come forth', or 'Raise him, O my Father', but acts
by his own authority.

44.—*And he that was dead came forth.*

The effect of our Lord's words was seen at once. As soon
as he 'cried', Lazarus was seen coming up out of the cave,
before the eyes of the crowd. A more plain, distinct, and
unmistakable miracle it would be impossible for man to
imagine. That a dead man should hear a voice, obey it, rise
up, and move forth from his grave alive, is utterly contrary
to nature. God alone could cause such a thing. What first
began life in him, how lungs and heart began to act again,
suddenly and instantaneously, it would be waste of time to
speculate. It was a miracle, and there we must leave it.

The idea of some, that Lazarus moved out of the grave
without the use of his legs, passing through air like a spirit or

ghost, seems to me needless and unreasonable. I agree with Hutcheson, Hall, and Pearce, that though 'bound hand and foot', there is no certain proof that his legs were tied together so tightly that he could not move out of the grave, though slowly and with difficulty, like one encumbered, on his own feet. The tardy shuffling action of such a figure would strike all. Pearce remarks, 'He must have come forth crawling on his knees.' We are surely not required to multiply miracles.—Yet the idea that Lazarus came out with a supernatural motion seems to be held by Augustine, Zwingle, Œcolampadius, Bucer, Gualter, Toletus, Jansenius, Lampe, Lightfoot, and Alford, who think it part of the miracle. I would not press my opinion positively on others, though I firmly maintain it. My own private feeling is that the slow, gradual, tottering movements of a figure encumbered by graveclothes would impress a crowd far more than the rapid ghost-like gliding out in air of a body, of which the feet did not move.

His face was bound about … napkin.

This is mentioned to show that he had been really dead, and his corpse treated like all other corpses. If not dead, he would have been unable to breathe through the napkin for four days.

Jesus saith … Loose him, and let him go.

This command was given for two reasons: partly that many around might touch Lazarus, and see for themselves that it was not a ghost, but a real body that was raised; partly that he might be able to walk to his own house before the eyes of the multitude, as a living man. This, until he was freed from graveclothes and his eyes were unbandaged, would have been impossible.

Very striking is it to remark how in the least minute particulars the objections of infidels and sceptics are quietly forestalled and met in Gospel narrative! Thus Chrysostom remarks that the command to 'loose him' would enable the friends who bore Lazarus to the grave, to know from the grave-clothes that it was the very person they had buried four days before. They would recognize the clothes: they could not say, as some had said in the case of the blind man, 'This is not he.' He also remarks that both hands, eyes, ears, and nostrils would all convince the witnesses of the truth of the miracle.

45.—Then many of the Jews … believed on him.

This verse describes the good effect which the raising of Lazarus had on many of the Jews who had come from Jerusalem to comfort Mary and Martha. Their remaining prejudices gave way. They were unable to resist the extra-ordinary evidence of the miracle they had just seen. From that day they no longer denied that Jesus was the Christ. Whether their belief was faith unto salvation may well be doubted: but at any rate they ceased to oppose and blaspheme. And it is more than probable that on the day of Pentecost many of those very Jews whose hearts had been prepared by the miracle of Bethany, came boldly forward and were baptized.

We should observe in this verse what a signal blessing God was pleased to bestow on sympathy and kindness. If the Jews had not come to comfort Mary under her affliction, they would not have seen the mighty miracle of raising Lazarus, and perhaps would not have been saved.

Lampe remarks on these Jews, 'They had come as the merciful, and they obtained mercy.'

Bessner observes the beautiful delicacy with which St John draws a veil over the effect on Martha and Mary of this miracle, while he dwells on the effect it had on strangers.

46.—*But some of them went … Pharisees, etc.*

We see in this verse the bad effect which the raising of Lazarus had on some who saw it. Instead of being softened and convinced, they were hardened and enraged. They were vexed to see even more unanswerable proofs that Jesus was the Christ, and irritated to feel that their own unbelief was more than ever inexcusable. They therefore hurried off to the Pharisees to report what they had seen, and to point out the progress that our Lord was making in the immediate neighbourhood of Jerusalem.

The amazing wickedness of human nature is strikingly illustrated in this verse. There is no greater mistake than to suppose that seeing miracles will necessarily convert souls. Here is a plain proof that it does not. Never was there a more remarkable confirmation of our Lord's words in the parable of the rich man and Lazarus: 'If they hear not Moses and the prophets, neither will they be persuaded, though one rose from the dead.'

Musculus observes what a wonderful example we have here of the sovereign grace of God, choosing some, and leading them to repentance and faith, and not choosing others. Here is the same miracle, seen under the same circumstances, and with the same evidence, by a large crowd of persons: yet while some believe, others believe not! It is like the case of the two thieves on the cross, both seeing the same sight, one repenting and the other impenitent. The same fire which melts wax hardens clay.

In leaving this wonderful miracle, there are three things which demand special notice.

(*a*) We should observe that we are not told of anything that Lazarus said about his state while in the grave, and nothing of his after-history. Tradition says that he lived for thirty years after, and was never known to smile: but this is probably a mere apocryphal invention. As to his silence, we can easily see there is a divine wisdom about it. If St Paul 'could not utter' the things that he saw in the third heaven, and called them 'unspeakable things', it is not strange that Lazarus should say nothing of what he saw in paradise (2 Cor. 12:4). But there may be always seen in Scripture a striking silence about the feelings of men and women who have been the subjects of remarkable divine interposition. God's ways are not man's ways. Man loves sensation and excitement, and likes to make God's work on his fellow-creatures a gazing-stock and a show, to their great damage. God almost always seems to withdraw them from the public, both for their own good and his glory.

(*b*) We should observe that we are told nothing of the feelings of Martha and Mary, after they saw their brother raised to life. The veil is drawn over their joy, though it was not over their sorrow. Affliction is a more profitable study than rejoicing.

(*c*) We should observe, lastly, that the raising of Lazarus is one of the most signal instances in the Gospels of Christ's divine power. To him who could work such a miracle nothing is impossible. He can raise from the death of sin any dead soul, however far gone and corrupt. He will raise us from the grave at his own second appearing. The voice which called Lazarus from the tomb is almighty. 'The dead shall hear the voice of the Son of God: and they that hear shall live' (John 5:25).

CHAPTER SIX

John 11:47-57

47 Then gathered the chief priests and the Pharisees a council, and said, What do we? for this man doeth many miracles.

48 If we let him thus alone, all men will believe on him: and the Romans shall come and take away both our place and nation.

49 And one of them, named Caiaphas, being the high priest that same year, said unto them, Ye know nothing at all,

50 Nor consider that it is expedient for us, that one man should die for the people, and that the whole nation perish not.

51 And this spake he not of himself: but being high priest that year, he prophesied that Jesus should die for that nation;

52 And not for that nation only, but that also he should gather together in one the children of God that were scattered abroad.

53 Then from that day forth they took counsel together for to put him to death.

54 Jesus therefore walked no more openly among the Jews; but went thence unto a country near to the wilderness, into a city called Ephraim, and there continued with his disciples.

55 And the Jews' passover was nigh at hand: and many went out of the country up to Jerusalem before the passover, to purify themselves.

56 Then sought they for Jesus, and spake among themselves, as they stood in the temple, What think ye, that he will not come to the feast?

57 Now both the chief priests and the Pharisees had given a
commandment, that, if any man knew where he were, he should
shew it, that they might take him.

THESE concluding verses of the eleventh chapter of St
John contain a melancholy picture of human nature.
As we turn away from Jesus Christ and the grave at Bethany,
and look at Jerusalem and the rulers of the Jews, we may
well say, 'Lord, what is man?'

We should observe, for one thing, in these verses, *the desperate wickedness of man's natural heart.* A mighty miracle
was wrought within an easy walk of Jerusalem. A man four
days dead was raised to life, in the sight of many witnesses.
The fact was unmistakable, and could not be denied; and
yet the chief priests and Pharisees would not believe that he
who did this miracle ought to be received as the Messiah.
In the face of overwhelming evidence they shut their eyes,
and refused to be convinced. 'This man', they admitted,
'does many miracles.' But so far from yielding to this testimony, they only plunged into further wickedness, and 'took
counsel to put him to death'. Great, indeed, is the power of
unbelief!

Let us beware of supposing that miracles alone have any
power to convert men's souls, and to make them Christians.
The idea is a complete delusion. To fancy, as some do, that
if they saw something wonderful done before their eyes in
confirmation of the gospel, they would at once cast off all
indecision and serve Christ, is a mere idle dream. It is the

grace of the Spirit in our hearts, and not miracles, that our souls require. The Jews of our Lord's day are a standing proof to mankind that men may see signs and wonders, and yet remain hard as stone. It is a deep and true saying, 'If [men] hear not Moses and the prophets, neither will they be persuaded, though one rose from the dead' (Luke 16:31).

We must never wonder if we see abounding unbelief in our own times, and around our own homes. It may seem at first inexplicable to us, how men cannot see the truth which seems so clear to ourselves, and do not receive the gospel which appears so worthy of acceptation. But the plain truth is, that man's unbelief is a far more deeply-seated disease than it is generally reckoned. It is proof against the logic of facts, against reasoning, against argument, against moral suasion. Nothing can melt it down but the grace of God. If we ourselves believe, we can never be too thankful. But we must never count it a strange thing, if we see many of our fellow-Christians just as hardened and unbelieving as the Jews.

We should observe, for another thing, *the blind ignorance with which God's enemies often act and reason.* These rulers of the Jews said to one another, 'If we let this Christ alone, we shall be ruined. If we do not stop his course, and make an end of his miracles, the Romans will interfere, and make an end of our nation.' Never, the event afterward proved, was there a more short-sighted and erring judgment than this. They rushed madly on the path they had chosen and the very thing they feared came to pass. They did not leave our Lord alone, but crucified and slew him. And what happened then? After a few years, the very calamity they had dreaded took place: the Roman armies did come, destroyed Jerusalem, burned the temple, and carried away the whole nation into captivity.

The well-read Christian need hardly be reminded of many suchlike things in the history of Christ's church. The Roman emperors persecuted the Christians in the first three centuries, and thought it a positive duty not to let them alone. But the more they persecuted them, the more they increased. The blood of the martyrs became the seed of the church.—The English Papists, in the days of Queen Mary, persecuted the Protestants, and thought that truth was in danger if they were let alone. But the more they burned our forefathers, the more they confirmed men's minds in steadfast attachment to the doctrines of the Reformation.—In short, the words of the second Psalm are continually verified in this world: 'The kings of the earth set themselves, and the rulers take counsel together, against the LORD'; but 'He that sitteth in the heavens shall laugh: the LORD shall have them in derision' (Psa. 2:2, 4). God can make the designs of his enemies work together for the good of his people, and cause the wrath of man to praise him. In days of trouble, and rebuke, and blasphemy, believers may rest patiently in the Lord. The very things that at one time seem likely to hurt them, shall prove in the end to be for their gain.

We should observe, lastly, *what importance bad men sometimes attach to outward ceremonial, while their hearts are full of sin*. We are told that many Jews 'went out of the country up to Jerusalem before the passover, to purify themselves'. The most of them, it may be feared, neither knew nor cared anything about inward purity of heart. They made much ado about the washings, and fasting, and ascetic observances, which formed the essence of popular Jewish religion in our Lord's time; and yet they were willing in a very few days to shed innocent blood. Strange as it may appear, these very sticklers for outward sanctification were found ready to do the will of the Pharisees, and to put their own Messiah to a violent death.

Extremes like this meeting together in the same person are unhappily far from uncommon. Experience shows that a bad conscience will often try to satisfy itself by a show of zeal for the cause of religion, while the 'weightier matters' of the faith are entirely neglected. The very same man who is ready to compass sea and land to attain ceremonial purity, is often the very man, who, if he had fit opportunity, would not shrink from helping to crucify Christ. Startling as these assertions may seem, they are abundantly borne out by plain facts. The cities where Lent is kept at this day with the most extravagant strictness are the very cities where the carnival before Lent is a season of glaring excess and immorality. The people in some parts of Christendom, who make much ado one week about fasting and priestly absolution, are the very people who another week will think nothing of murder! These things are simple realities. The hideous inconsistency of the Jewish formalists in our Lord's time has never been without a long succession of followers.

Let us settle it firmly in our minds that a religion which expends itself in zeal for outward formalities is utterly worthless in God's sight. The purity that God desires to see is not the purity of bodily washing and fasting, of holy water and self-imposed asceticism, but purity of heart. Will-worship and ceremonialism may 'satisfy the flesh', but they do not tend to promote real godliness. The standard of Christ's kingdom must be sought in the Sermon on the Mount: 'Blessed are the pure in heart: for they shall see God' (Matt. 5:8; Col. 2:23).

NOTES ON JOHN 11:47-57

47.—Then gathered ... priests ... Pharisees a council.

This council was probably the great Sanhedrin, or consultative assembly of the Jewish church. It was for purely ecclesiastical, and not for civil or political purposes. It is the same assembly before which, it is conjectured with much show of reason, our Lord made his defence, in the fifth chapter of this Gospel. On receiving the tidings of the astounding miracle which had been wrought at Bethany, our Lord's bitterest enemies, the chief priests and Pharisees, seem to have been alarmed and enraged, and to have felt the absolute necessity of taking decided measures to check our

Lord's progress. Ecclesiastical rulers, unhappily, are often the foremost enemies of the gospel.

And said, What do we?

This question indicates perplexity and irritation. 'What are we about? Are we going to sit still, and let this new Teacher carry all before him? What is the use of trifling with this new heresy? We are doing nothing effectual to check it. It grows: and we let it alone.'

For this man doeth many miracles.

This is a marvellous admission. Even our Lord's worst enemies confess that our Lord did miracles, and many miracles. Can we doubt that they would have denied the truth of his miracles, if they could? But they do not seem to have attempted it. They were too many, too public, and too thoroughly witnessed, for them to dare to deny them. How, in the face of this fact, modern infidels and sceptics can talk of our Lord's miracles as being impostures and delusions, they would do well to explain! If the Pharisees who lived in our Lord's time, and who moved heaven and earth to oppose his progress, never dared to dispute the fact that he worked miracles, it is useless to begin denying his miracles now, after eighteen centuries have passed away.

Let us note the desperate hardness and wickedness of man's heart. Even the sight of miracles will not convert anyone without the renewing grace of the Holy Ghost.

Brentius remarks that the simple answer to the question of this verse ought to have been, 'Our duty is to believe at once that this worker of many miracles is the Christ of God.'

48.—If we let him thus alone.

This means, 'If we continue to treat him as we do now, and take no more active measures to put him down; if we only dispute, and reason, and argue, and cavil, and denounce him, but let him have his liberty, let him go where he pleases, let him do what he pleases, and preach what he pleases.'

'Thus' can only mean 'as at present, and hitherto'.

All men will believe on him.

This means the bulk of the population will believe that he is what he *professes* to be,—the promised Messiah. The number of his adherents will increase, and faith in his Messiahship will become contagious, and spread all over Palestine.

The word 'all', in this sentence, must evidently not be taken literally. It only means 'the great mass of the people.' It is like 'all men come to him', said by the angry disciples of John the Baptist about Christ (John 3:26). When men lose their tempers, and talk in passion, they are very apt to use exaggerated expressions.

The Romans ... come ... take away ... place ... nation.

The process of reasoning by which the Pharisees arrived at this conclusion was probably something of this kind. 'This man, if let alone, will gather round him a crowd of adherents, who will proclaim him a Leader and King. This our governors, the Romans, will hear, and consider it a rebellion against their authority. Then they will send an army, deal with us as rebels, destroy Jerusalem and the temple, and carry away the whole Jewish nation, as the Babylonians did, into captivity.'

In this wretched argument it is difficult to say which appears most prominent, ignorance or unbelief.

It was an *ignorant* argument. The Pharisees ought to have known well that nothing was further from our Lord's teaching than the idea of an earthly kingdom, supported by an armed force. He always proclaimed that his kingdom was not of this world, and not temporal, like Solomon's or David's. He had never hinted at any deliverance from Roman authority. He distinctly taught men to render to Cæsar the things that were Cæsar's, and had distinctly refused, when appealed to, to be 'a Judge or divider' among the Jews. Such a person, therefore, was not the least likely to excite the jealousy of the Romans.

It was an *unbelieving* argument. The Pharisees ought to have believed that the Romans could never have conquered and put down our Lord and his adherents, if he really was the Messiah, and could work miracles at his will. The Philistines could not overcome David, and the Romans could not have overcome David's greater Son. By their own showing, the Jewish nation would have had protection enough in the miracle-working power of our Lord.

That there was an expectation throughout the East, at the time of our Lord's ministry, that some remarkable person was about to arise, and become a great leader, is mentioned by Roman historians. But there is no evidence that the Roman government ever showed jealousy of anyone who was merely a religious teacher, like our Lord, and did not interfere with the civil power.

The plain truth is, that this saying of the Pharisees looks like an excuse, caught up as a weapon against our Lord, and a pretext for stirring up enmity against him. What they really hated was our Lord's doctrine, which exposed their own system, and weakened their authority. They felt that 'their craft was in danger'. But not daring to say this publicly, they pretended a fear that he would excite the jealousy of the Romans, and endanger the whole nation. They did just the same when they finally accused him to Pilate, as One that stirred up sedition, and made himself a King. It is no uncommon thing for wicked people to assign very untrue reasons for their conduct, and to keep back and conceal their true motives. Demetrius, and his friends at Ephesus, said that the temple of the great goddess Diana was in danger, when in reality it was their own 'craft' and their own 'wealth'. The Jews at Thessalonica who persecuted Paul, pretended great zeal for 'the decrees of Cæsar', when their real motive was hatred of Christ's gospel. The Pharisees here pretended fear of the Romans, when in reality they found the growing influence of Jesus pulling down their own power over the people.

Calvin observes, 'They double their wickedness by a plausible disguise,—their zeal for the public good. The fear that chiefly distressed them was, that their own tyranny should be destroyed: but they pretend to be anxious about the temple and worship of God.'

Bucer compares the Pharisees' pretended fear of the Romans to the absurd fears of the consequence of printing and literature, which the Papists used to express at the period of the Reformation.

Flacius remarks, that 'through fear of Cæsar, God is despised and his Son crucified, and this under pretext of preserving religion, the temple, and the nation. Human wisdom preserves itself by appeasing man and offending God!'

Ferus remarks that the council entirely forgot that 'Rulers, whether the Romans or any others, are not a terror to good works, but to evil. If the Jews had believed and obeyed God, they had nothing to fear.'

That the leading Jews at Jerusalem had a strong suspicion that Jesus really was the Messiah, in spite of all their outrageous enmity and unbelief, is evident not only from comparison of other places, but from their nervous anxiety to get rid of him. They knew that Daniel's seventy weeks were run out. They could not deny the miracles that Jesus did. But they dared not follow out their convictions, and draw the conclusion they ought to have drawn. They willingly shut their eyes against light.

How miserably mistaken the policy of the Pharisees proved to be, it is needless to say. If they had let Jesus alone, and allowed his gospel to be received and believed, Jerusalem, humanly speaking, might have stood to this day, and the Jews might have been more mighty and prosperous than in the days of Solomon. By not letting Jesus alone, and by killing him, they filled up the measure of their nation's sin, and brought destruction on the temple, and scattering on the whole people.

'Take away', applied to place here, must mean 'destroy'. Thus Matthew 24:39: 'The flood … took them all away.'

Some, as Heinsius and Bloomfield, think that 'our place' means the city, Jerusalem.

Some, as Olshausen and Alford, think that 'our place' means 'our country'.

Others, as Maldonatus, Hutcheson, Poole, and Hammond, with whom I entirely agree, think 'our place' means the temple (compare Acts 6:13, 14). Lampe thinks this view is proved by Micah 1:3.

Calvin observes how many people in his day were always hanging back from helping the Protestant Reformation, from the very same motives as these Jews,—the fear of consequences. 'We must consult public tranquillity. There are dangers in the way.'

49.—*And one of them, named Caiaphas.*

This man, by comparing Acts 5:17, would seem to have been of the sect of the Sadducees. We also know that he was son-in-law to Annas, of whom Josephus specially mentions that he was a Sadducee. If this view be correct (and Guyse, Gill, Scott, and Lampe agree with me in it), it rather accounts for the contemptuous way in which he seems to speak in replying here to the saying of the Pharisees. It is remarkable, however, to observe how Pharisees and Sadducees, who disagreed on so many points, were agreed in hating and opposing Christ. Formalists and sceptics, in all ages, make common cause against the gospel.

Being … high priest … same year.

This expression shows the disorder and irregularity which prevailed in the Jewish church in our Lord's time. According to the law of Moses, the office of high priest was tenable for life. In the last days of the Jews, the office seems to have been obtainable by election, and to have been held with great variety of term. Caiaphas was high priest when John the Baptist began his ministry, and Annas with him (Luke 3:2). He was also high priest after the day of Pentecost, and before the persecution of Stephen. No wonder St Paul says, on a subsequent occasion, of Ananias, 'I wist not . . . that he was the high priest' (Acts 23:2-5).

Poole remarks, 'After Herod's time there was no regard to the family of Aaron, but the Romans made what high priests they pleased. Josephus tells us that the Jews had thirteen high priests from Aaron to Solomon, which was

612 years; eighteen from Solomon to the Babylonian captivity, which was 460 years; fifteen from the captivity to Antiochus, which was 414 years: but they had no fewer than twenty-eight between the time that Herod began to reign and Jerusalem was destroyed, which was less than a century.'

Said … Ye know nothing at all.

The word rendered 'ye' is here emphatic in the Greek. It seems not unlikely that it expresses Caiaphas' contempt for the ignorance and helplessness of the Pharisees' question. 'You and all your party do not understand what the situation of things requires. You are wasting time in complaints and expressions of vexation, when a sterner, severer policy is imperatively demanded.'

Chrysostom remarks, 'What others made matter of doubt, and put forth in the way of deliberation, this man cried aloud shamelessly, openly, and audaciously. *One must die.*'

Pearce thinks that some of the Jews in council must have talked of only putting a stop to Christ's preaching, as they afterwards tried to stop the apostles (Acts 4:18), but that Caiaphas ridiculed such weak counsel, and advised more violent measures. May we not suppose that Nicodemus and others spoke in favour of our Lord?

50.—Nor consider.

The word thus rendered is almost always translated 'reason', and is nowhere 'consider', except here. It seems to imply that Caiaphas wished the Pharisees to know that they had not reasoned out and properly weighed the right thing to be done. Hence this perplexity. He would now show them the conclusion they ought to have come to.

It is expedient ... one ... die ... whole ... perish not.

Caiaphas' conclusion is short and decisive. He gives it elliptically. 'This man must die. It is far better that one should die, whether innocent or not, for the benefit of the whole nation, than that the whole nation should be brought into trouble and perish. You are thinking that if we do not let this man alone, and interfere, we are injuring an innocent person. Away with such childish scruples. Let him be put out of the way. It is expedient to kill him. Better he should die to save the nation from further trouble, than live, and the nation be brought into trouble by him.'

I cannot suppose that Caiaphas meant anything more than this. He simply argues that Christ's death would be a public benefit, and that to spare him might bring destruction on the nation. Of the full meaning that his words were capable of bearing, I do not believe he had the least idea.

Let us carefully note here what crimes and sins may be committed on the ground of *expediency*. None are so likely to be tempted to commit such sins as rulers and governors. None are so likely to do things unjust, dishonest, and oppressive, as a government under the pressure of the spurious argument that it is 'expedient' that the few should suffer, rather than the many should take harm. For political expediency Christ was crucified. What a fact that is! Ought we not rather to ask always what is just, what is right, what is honourable in the sight of God? That which is morally wrong can never be politically right. To govern only for the sake of pleasing and benefiting the majority, without any reference to the eternal principles of justice, right, and mercy, may be *expedient*, and please man; but it does not please God.

Calvin observes, 'Let us learn never to separate what is useful and expedient from what is lawful, since we ought not to expect any prosperity and success but from the blessing of God.'

Œcolampadius remarks that we must never do evil that good may come. 'If you could, by the slaying of one good man, work the saving of many, it would be unlawful.'

Poole observes, 'Never was anything spoken more diabolically. Like a wretched politician, concerned for nothing but the people's safety, Caiaphas saith not "it is lawful," but "it is expedient" for us that one man, be he never so good, never so innocent and just, should die.'

Doddridge remarks, 'When will the politicians of this world learn to trust God in his own ways, rather than to trust themselves and their own wisdom, in violation of all rules of truth, honour, and conscience?'

51, 52.—*And this spake he not of himself, etc.*

These two verses contain a parenthetical comment by St John, on the address of Caiaphas to the Pharisees. It is a peculiar passage, and not without difficulty. That a man like Caiaphas should be said to prophesy, and that his prophecy should be of so wide and extensive a character, is undoubtedly strange. I offer a few remarks that may help to throw light on the passage.

That God can employ a wicked man to declare prophetical truth, is clearly proved by the case of Balaam. But the positions of Balaam and Caiaphas were very different.

That the Jewish high priest at any time possessed, by virtue of his office, the power of predicting things to come, I can nowhere find. David certainly speaks of Zadok as 'a seer' (2 Sam. 15:27). The high priest's ephod conveyed a certain mysterious power to the wearer, of foreseeing things immediately near (1 Sam. 23:9). The 'urim and thummin', whatever they were, which dwelt in the breast-plate of the high priest, appear to have given the wearer peculiar powers of discernment. But even they were withdrawn at the destruction of the first temple. In short, there is an utter absence of proof that a Jewish high priest, in the time of our Lord, had any power of prophesying.

I believe that the verses before us are very elliptical, and require much to be supplied in order to convey the meaning of St John. The only satisfactory sense I can put upon the passage will be found in the following free paraphrase.

This spake he not of himself.

He spoke these words, though he was not aware of it, under the influence of an overruling power, making him say things of far deeper meaning than he was conscious of himself. As Œcolampadius says, 'God used him as an instrument' (see Isa. 10:15).

But being high priest that year, he prophesied.

He spoke words which as the event showed afterwards, were eminently prophetical: and the fact that they fell from his lips when he was high priest, made them more remarkable, when afterwards remembered and noted.

That Jesus should die for that nation.

He actually foretold, though the fulfilment was in a manner very different from his intentions, that Jesus would die for the benefit of the Jewish nation.

And not for that nation only, etc.

And he also foretold what was practically fulfilled afterwards, though in a way marvellously unlike what he thought,—that Jesus would not only die for the Jewish nation, but for the benefit of all God's children at present scattered all over the world.

The utmost, in fact, that I can make of John's explanatory comment, is that he remarks on the extraordinary manner in which Caiaphas' words proved true, though in a way that he never intended, wished, or expected. He lets fall a saying on a great public occasion, which comes from his lips with great authority, on account of his office as high priest. That saying was afterwards fulfilled in the most marvellous manner by the overruling providence of God, but in a way that the speaker never dreamed of. The thing was afterwards remembered and remarked on; and it seemed, says St John, as if being high priest that year, he was miraculously compelled by the Holy Ghost to prophesy the redemption of mankind, at the very time that he thought he was only speaking of putting Christ to death. Caiaphas in short meant nothing but to advise the murder of Christ. But the Holy Ghost obliged him unconsciously to use words which were a most remarkable prediction of Christ's death bringing life to a lost world.

The Greek word rendered 'should die' would be more literally, 'was about to die'. It simply expresses a future coming event.

The 'children of God scattered abroad', I believe, means the elect of God among the Gentiles. They are put in contrast with 'that nation', or 'the nation', as it would be more literally rendered.

The 'gathering together in one', I believe to be that final gathering of all Christ's members which is yet to come at his second advent (see Eph. 1:10; John 12:32; Gen. 49:10).

Lightfoot says, the Jews thought the greatest work of Messiah was to be the 'reduction, or gathering together of the captivities'.

I leave the passage with a very deep sense of its difficulty, and desire not to press my views on others dogmatically, if they are not satisfied with them.

Chrysostom remarks, 'Caiaphas prophesied, not knowing what he said; and the grace of God merely made use of his mouth, but touched not his accursed heart.'

Musculus and Ferus remark how striking the resemblance is between Caiaphas unintentionally using language fulfilled in a sense totally unlike what he meant, and the Jews saying of Christ to Pilate, 'His blood be on us and on our children.' They little knew the awful and tremendous extent of the saying.

The absurdity of the Roman Catholic claim, that the Pope's words and decrees are to be received as partially inspired because of his office, on the ground of this passage, is noted and exposed by all the Protestant commentators of the seventeenth century.

Lightfoot thinks we should lay great emphasis on the expression 'that same year', and justly so.—He observes that it was the very year when the high priest's office ended, and the veil was rent, and the Jewish dispensation wound up, and the Mosaic priesthood abrogated by Christ's becoming manifestly our priest.—He thinks St Paul, in Acts 23:5, 'I wist not that he was the high priest' may have meant 'that he did not know there was any high priest at all'.—He also observes that this very year at Pentecost, the Holy Ghost was poured out as the spirit of prophecy and revelation in an extraordinary measure. What wonder if 'that year' the last high priest, like Balaam, should prophesy.

53.—*Then from that day … counsel … death.*

We see here the result of Caiaphas' counsel. His stern, bold, outspoken proposal carried all the council with him, and even if Gamaliel, Nicodemus, and Joseph were there, their voices were silenced. From that very day it became a settled thing with the Jewish leaders at Jerusalem, that Jesus was to be put to death. The only difficulty was to find the way, the time, and the means of doing it, without creating a tumult. The great miracle just wrought at Bethany would doubtless increase the number of our Lord's adherents, and make it necessary to use caution in carrying out the murderous plan.

The conclusions of great ecclesiastical councils are seldom wise and good, and sometimes are wicked and cruel. Bold, forward, unscrupulous men, like Caiaphas, generally silence the quieter members, and carry all before them.

54.—*Jesus therefore walked … Jews.*

From this time our Lord found it necessary to give up appearing openly at Jerusalem, and came there no more till the week of his crucifixion. He knew the result of the council just held, either from his own divine knowledge, or from the information of friends like Nicodemus; and as his time was not fully come, he retired from Judæa for a season.

The expression 'no more', is literally 'not yet'. It must mean 'no more at present'.

May we not learn from our Lord's conduct, that it may be a duty sometimes not to court danger or death? There are seasons when it is a duty to retire, as well as seasons for going forward. There are times to be silent, as well as times to speak.

Hutcheson remarks, 'It is lawful for Christ's servants to flee when their death is decreed by enemies, and the persecution is personal.'

Went thence … wilderness … Ephraim … disciples.

Nothing whatever is known for certain of the distinct locality to which our Lord retired, or of the city here named. It seems, purposely, to have been a quiet, isolated, and little-frequented place. The probability is that it was beyond Jordan, in Perea, because when our Lord came to Jerusalem the last time he passed through Jericho.

Ellicott suggests that Ephraim was a town called also Ophrah, about twenty miles north of Jerusalem, on the borders of Samaria. He also thinks that on leaving Ephraim those words of St Luke (chapter 17:11) come in, which say that our Lord 'passed through the midst of Samaria and Galilee'. After that he thinks he went through Perea, to Jericho. But I am not satisfied that he proves these points.

It is worth noticing that our Lord chose a scene of entire quiet and seclusion as his last abode, before going up to his last great season of suffering at the crucifixion. It is well to get alone and be still, before we take in hand any great work for God. Our Saviour was not above this. How much more should his disciples remember it! In saying this, I would not be thought to commend the ostentatious 'retreats' of the Romish Church and its followers. It is of the very essence of Christian retirement, if it is to be profitable, that it should be without parade, and should not attract the notice of men. The life of the Eremite has no warrant in Scripture.

When it says that our Lord continued or tarried at Ephraim 'with his disciples', it is worth noticing that we do not hear a word of any public works that he did there. It looks as if he devoted the last few quiet days that remained before his crucifixion, to uninterrupted communion with the Father, and private instruction of his disciples.

55.—And ... Jews' passover ... nigh at hand.

This expression, like many others in John's Gospel, shows that he wrote for the church generally, and for many readers who were not familiar with Jewish feasts and customs.

And many went ... country ... before ... passover.

This seems mentioned as a simple matter of custom among the Jews, and not as a thing done this year more than any other. They always did so; and thus drew together, for seven days before the passover, a larger collection of people at Jerusalem than at any other time of the year. Hence the crowds and expectation when our Lord appeared. He had been talked of by people from all parts of Palestine.

To purify themselves.

This refers to the ceremonial washings, purifications, and atonements for ceremonial uncleanness, which all strict Jews were careful to go through before eating the passover (see 2 Chron. 30:18, 19). It is impossible to read the book of Leviticus carefully, and not to be struck with the almost endless number of ways in which an Israelite could become ceremonially unclean, and need going to the priest to have an atonement made (see Num. 9:6-11). That the Pharisees, in such matters, added to legal strictness by their absurd

THE POWER AND SYMPATHY OF CHRIST

scrupulosity, such as 'straining out a gnat', as if the dead body of such an insect could defile them, we cannot doubt: but the simple law as it stood was a yoke that was very hard to bear. No wonder that thousands of devout Jews came anxiously before the passover to Jerusalem, to be made ceremonially clean and fit for the feast.

It is worth noting how singularly particular men are sometimes about forms and ceremonies and outward correctness, while they coolly plan and execute enormous crimes. The Jews, zealous about 'purifying' themselves while they were planning the murder of Christ, have had imitators and followers in every age of the church. Strictness about forms and ceremonies, and utter recklessness about gross sin, are found quite compatible in many hearts.

56.—Then sought they … Jesus, and spake, etc., etc.

The persons here mentioned seem to me to have been the Jews from all parts of Palestine, mentioned in the last verse, who had come up to prepare for the passover. The fame and history of our Lord were probably so great throughout Palestine, that one of the first inquiries the comers would make of one another would be about him. And as they stood in the temple court, waiting for their turn to go through ceremonial purification, or talking with old friends and acquaintances who had come up, like themselves, from the country, Jesus would probably be a principal topic of conversation.

What think ye, that … not come … feast?

This is mentioned as one of the principal inquiries made by the Jews of one another. Our Lord, on a former occasion, had not come up to the passover (see John 6).

They might, therefore, naturally feel doubtful whether he would come now.

It is noteworthy that the question admits of being taken as one, or divided into two distinct ones.

Some think that it means, 'What think ye of the question, whether he will come to the feast or not?'

Others hold that it means, 'What think ye of Christ, and especially of his position at this time? Do you think that he will not come to the feast?' I myself prefer this view.

It is noteworthy that the very question with which our Lord confounded the Pharisees a few days after, as recorded in St Matthew 22:42, begins with precisely the same Greek words as those here used, 'What think ye of Christ?'

57.—*Now both ... priests ... Pharisees, etc., etc.*

This verse shows the first steps which had been taken after the session of the council which adopted the advice of Caiaphas to kill Jesus. A general order had been given that if any man knew where Jesus lodged in Jerusalem, he was to give information, in order that he might be apprehended.

I cannot help thinking myself that this order must only have referred to Jerusalem, and the house where our Lord might lodge when he came to the passover, if he did come. I cannot suppose that our Lord's enemies could be ignorant where he was between the miracle of Bethany and the passover. But I fancy they dared not run the risk of a tumult or rebellion, which might be caused if they sent into the rural districts to apprehend him. Indeed, it is doubtful whether the jurisdiction of the priests and Pharisees extended beyond the walls of Jerusalem, and whether they could lay hands upon our Lord anywhere outside the city. This may have been the reason why he often lodged at Bethany.

Musculus here discusses the question, whether obedience to the powers that be, obliges us to give up a man to those who are seeking to apprehend him. He answers, 'Decidedly not; if we believe him to be an innocent man.'

Select Hymns

(1) PHIL. 1:23.

I journey forth rejoicing
  From this dark vale of tears,
To heav'nly joy, and freedom
  From earthly bonds and fears;
Where Christ our Lord shall gather
  All His redeemed again,
His kingdom to inherit;—
  Good night, till then!

Go to thy quiet resting,
  Poor tenement of clay!
From all thy pain and weakness
  I gladly haste away;
But still in faith confiding
  To find thee yet again,
All glorious and immortal;—
  Good night, till then!

Why thus so sadly weeping,
   Beloved ones of my heart?
The Lord is good and gracious,
   Though now He bids us part.
Oft have we met in gladness,
   And we shall meet again,
All sorrow left behind us;—
   Good night, till then!

I go to see His glory
   Whom we have loved below;
I go, the blessèd angels,
   The holy saints to know;
Our lovely ones departed,
   I go to find again,
I wait for you to join us;—
   Good night, till then!

I hear the Saviour calling:
   The joyful hour is come;
The angel guards are ready,
   To guide me to our home,
Where Christ, our Lord, shall gather
   All His redeemed again,
His kingdom to inherit;—
   Good night, till then!

From *Hymns from the Land of Luther.*

(2) Col. 1:19.

I lay my sins on Jesus,
    The spotless Lamb of God;
He bears them all, and frees us
    From the accursèd load.
I bring my guilt to Jesus,
    To wash my crimson stains
White in His blood most precious,
    Till not a spot remains.

I lay my wants on Jesus;
    All fullness dwells in Him;
He heals all my diseases,
    He doth my soul redeem.
I lay my griefs on Jesus,
    My burdens and my cares;
He from them all releases;
    He all my sorrows shares.

I rest my soul on Jesus,
    This weary soul of mine;
His right hand me embraces,
    I on His breast recline.
I love the name of Jesus,
    Immanuel, Christ, the Lord;
Like fragrance on the breezes
    His name abroad is poured.

I long to be like Jesus,
    Meek, loving, lowly, mild;
I long to be like Jesus,
    The Father's holy child;
I long to be with Jesus,
    Amid the heavenly throng;
To sing with saints His praises,
    To learn the angels' song.

H. BONAR

(3) 1 PET. 5:7.

Lord, it belongs not to my care
    Whether I die or live:
To love and serve Thee is my share,
    And this Thy grace must give.

If life be long, I will be glad,
    That I may long obey;
If short, yet why should I be sad
    To soar to endless day?

Christ leads me through no darker rooms
    Than He went through before;
He that unto God's kingdom comes,
    Must enter by His door.

Come, Lord, when grace hath made me meet
    Thy blessèd face to see;
For if Thy work on earth be sweet,
    What will Thy glory be!

Then shall I end my sad complaints,
    And weary, sinful days,
And join with the triumphant saints
    That sing Jehovah's praise.

My knowledge of that life is small,
    The eye of faith is dim;
But 'tis enough that Christ knows all,
    And I shall bc with Him.

R. BAXTER

(4) JOHN 6:37.

Just as I am, without one plea,
    But that Thy blood was shed for me,
And that Thou bid'st me come to Thee,
    O Lamb of God, I come!

Just as I am, and waiting not
    To rid my soul of one dark blot,
To Thee, whose blood can cleanse each spot,
    O Lamb of God, I come!

Just as I am, though tossed about
  With many a conflict, many a doubt,
Fightings within, and fears without,
  O Lamb of God, I come!

Just as I am, poor, wretched, blind:
  Sight, riches, healing of the mind,
Yes, all I need, in Thee to find,
  O Lamb of God, I come!

Just as I am, Thou wilt receive,
  Wilt welcome, pardon, cleanse, relieve,
Because Thy promise I believe,
  O Lamb of God, I come!

Just as I am, Thy love unknown
  Has broken every barrier down,
Now, to be Thine, yea, Thine alone,
  O Lamb of God, I come!

CHARLOTTE ELLIOTT

(5) MATT. 11:28.

I heard the voice of Jesus say,
  'Come unto Me, and rest;
Lay down, thou weary one, lay down
  Thy head upon My breast.'

I came to Jesus as I was,
　　Weary, and worn, and sad;
I found in Him a resting-place,
　　And He has made me glad.

I heard the voice of Jesus say,
　　'Behold, I freely give
The living water;—thirsty one,
　　Stoop down, and drink, and live.'
I came to Jesus, and I drank
　　Of that life-giving stream;
My thirst was quenched, my soul revived,
　　And now I live in Him.

I heard the voice of Jesus say,
　　'I am this dark world's Light;
Look unto Me, thy morn shall rise,
　　And all thy day be bright.'
I looked to Jesus, and I found
　　In Him my Star, my Sun;
And in that Light of life I'll walk
　　Till travelling days are done.

H. BONAR

(6) PHIL. 1:21.

Rejoice for a brother deceased:
    Our loss is his infinite gain;
A soul out of prison released,
    And freed from its bodily chain.
With songs let us follow his flight,
    And mount with his spirit above;
Escaped to the mansions of light,
    And lodged in the Eden of love.

Our brother the haven hath gained,
    Out-flying the tempest and wind;
His rest he hath sooner obtained,
    And left his companions behind;
Still toss'd on a sea of distress,
    Hard-toiling to make the blest shore,
Where all is assurance and peace,
    And sorrow and sin are no more.

There all the ship's company meet,
    Who sailed with the Saviour beneath;
With shouting each other they greet,
    And triumph o'er sorrow and death:
The voyage of life's at an end,
    The mortal affliction is past:
The age that in heaven they spend
    For ever and ever shall last.

C. WESLEY

(7) Rev. 14:13.

How blest is our sister, bereft
    Of all that could burden her mind!
How easy the soul that has left
    This wearisome body behind!
This earth is affected no more
    With sickness, or shaken with pain:
The war in the members is o'er,
    And never shall vex her again.

This languishing head is at rest,
    Its thinking and aching are o'er;
This quiet immoveable breast
    Is heaved by affliction no more:
This heart is no longer the seat
    Of trouble and torturing pain;
It ceases to flutter and beat,
    It never shall flutter again.

The eyes she so seldom could close,
    By suff'ring forbidden to sleep,
Sealed up in their mortal repose,
    Have strangely forgotten to weep:
She is dwelling with Jesus in light,
    Where sickness and death are unknown;
Faith and hope are at last changed for sight,
    And her cross is laid down for a crown.

C. WESLEY

(8) JOHN 17:24.

Let me be with Thee where Thou art,
    My Saviour, my eternal rest;
Then only will this longing heart
    Be fully and for ever blessed.

Let me be with Thee where Thou art,
    Thy unveiled glory to behold;
Then only will this wand'ring heart
    Cease to be false to Thee and cold.

Let me be with Thee where Thou art,
    Where spotless saints Thy name adore;
Then only will this sinful heart
    Be evil and defiled no more.

Let me be with Thee where Thou art,
    Where none can die, where none remove;
There neither death nor life will part
    Me from Thy presence and Thy love.

CHARLOTTE ELLIOTT

(9) ROM. 13:11.

One sweetly solemn thought
    Comes to me, o'er and o'er:
I am nearer home today
    Than I ever have been before;

Nearer my Father's house,
    Where the many mansions be;
Nearer the great white throne;
    Nearer the crystal sea;

Nearer the bound of life,
    Where we lay our burdens down;
Nearer leaving the cross;
    Nearer gaining the crown.

But lying darkly between,
    Winding down through the night,
Is the deep and unknown stream,
    To be crossed ere we reach the light.

Jesus, perfect my trust!
    Strengthen the hand of my faith;
Let me feel Thee near when I stand
    On the edge of the shore of death;—

Feel Thee near when my feet
    Are slipping over the brink;
For it may be I'm nearer home—
    Nearer now than I think.

P. CAREY

(10) Rev. 1:5-7.

A few more years shall roll,
  A few more seasons come,
And we shall lie with them that rest
  Asleep within the tomb;
Then, O my Lord, prepare
  My soul for that great day;
O wash me in Thy precious blood,
  And take my sins away.

A few more suns shall set
  O'er these dark hills of time,
And we shall be where suns are not—
  A far serener clime.
Then, O my Lord, prepare
  My soul for that blest day;
O wash me in Thy precious blood,
  And take my sins away.

A few more storms shall beat
  On this wild rocky shore,
And we shall be where tempests cease,
  And surges swell no more.
Then, O my Lord, prepare
  My soul for that calm day;
O wash me in Thy precious blood,
  And take my sins away.

A few more struggles here,
  A few more partings o'er,
A few more toils, a few more tears,
  And we shall weep no more:
Then, O my Lord, prepare
  My soul for that blest day;
Oh, wash me in Thy precious blood,
  And take my sins away.

A few more Sabbaths here
  Shall cheer us on our way,
And we shall reach the endless rest,
  The eternal Sabbath-day.
Then, O my Lord, prepare
  My soul for that sweet day;
Oh, wash me in Thy precious blood,
  And take my sins away.

'Tis but a little while,
  And He shall come again,
Who died that we might live, who lives
  That we with Him may reign;
Then, O my Lord, prepare
  My soul for that glad day;
Oh, wash me in Thy precious blood,
  And take my sins away.

                    H. BONAR

(11) Job 3:18.

Lie down, frail body, here:
  Earth has no fairer bed,
No gentler pillow to afford;
  Come, rest thy home-sick head.

Lie down, with all thy aches:
  There is no aching here;
How soon shall all thy life-long ills
  For ever disappear!

Through these well-guarded gates
  No foe can entrance gain;
No sickness wastes, nor once intrudes
  The memory of pain.

Foot-sore and worn thou art,
  Breathless with toil and fight;
How welcome now the long-sought rest
  Of this all-tranquil night!

Rest for the toiling hand;
  Rest for the thought-worn brow;
Rest for the weary, way-sore feet;
  Rest from all labour now!

Rest for the fevered brain;
  Rest for the throbbing eye:
Though these parched lips of thine no more
  Shall pass the moan or sigh!

Soon shall the trump of God
    Give out the welcome sound,
That shakes thy silent chamber-walls,
    And breaks the turf-sealed ground.

'Ye dwellers in the dust,
    Awake: come forth, and sing;
Sharp has your frost of winter been,
    But bright shall be your spring.

'Twas sown in weakness here;
    'Twill then be raised in power.
That which was sown an earthly seed
    Shall rise a heavenly flower.'

H. BONAR

(12) JOHN 14:2.

Going home, and going quickly:
    'Tis a thought to cheer the heart!
Should we suffer, be it meekly;
    Soon the world and we must part
Never more to meet again;
    There's an end of suffering then,
There's an end of all that grieves us;
    How the thought of this relieves us!

Going home! How sweet the cheering,
　　Going to the place we love:
There in royal state appearing
　　'Mid the shining court above.
There our Father lives and reigns,
　　Greater He than fancy feigns;
There His people live for ever,
　　There's a portion failing never.

Going home! There's nothing dearer
　　To the pilgrim's heart than home;
Drawing nearer still, and nearer
　　To the place where pilgrims come.
Much he thinks of what will be,
　　Much of what he hopes to see;
Thinks of kindred, friends, and brothers,
　　But of Christ above all others.

'Tis the blessèd hope of seeing
　　Him he loves in glory there,
Blessèd hope of ever being
　　With the Lord, His joys to share;
'Tis the hope which lightens toil,
　　And in sorrow makes him smile,
Cheers him in the midst of strangers,
　　Keeps him when beset with dangers.

Going home! Then it behoves us
    Here to live as strangers do;
When the trial comes, it proves us,
    Proves if we have faith or no.
Let us make the promise sure,
    Let us to the end endure,
In the Saviour's love abiding
    In the Saviour's strength confiding.

              J. KELLY

(13) REV. 21:4.

Beyond the smiling and the weeping,
        I shall be soon;
Beyond the waking and the sleeping,
Beyond the sowing and the reaping,
        I shall be soon.
  Love, rest, and home!
  Sweet hope!
  Lord, tarry not, but come!

Beyond the blooming and the fading,
        I shall be soon;
Beyond the shining and the shading,
Beyond the hoping and the dreading,
        I shall be soon.
  Love, rest, and home! etc.

Beyond the rising and the setting,
    I shall be soon;
Beyond the calming and the fretting,
Beyond remembering and forgetting,
    I shall be soon.
    Love, rest, and home! etc.

Beyond the gathering and the strewing
    I shall be soon;
Beyond the ebbing and the flowing,
Beyond the coming and the going,
    I shall be soon.
    Love, rest, and home! etc.

Beyond the parting and the meeting,
    I shall be soon;
Beyond the farewell and the greeting,
Beyond the pulse's fever-beating,
    I shall be soon.
    Love, rest, and home! etc.

H. BONAR

(14) EPH. 3:15.

Come, let us join our friends above
    That have made sure the prize;
And on the eagle wings of love,
    To joy celestial rise.

Let all the saints terrestrial sing
    With those to glory gone;
For all the servants of our King,
    In earth and heaven are one.

One family, we dwell in Him,
    One church, above, beneath;
Though now divided by the stream,
    The narrow stream of death.

One army of the living God,
    To His command we bow;
Part of His host hath crossed the flood,
    And part is crossing now.

Ten thousand to their endless home
    Each moment pass away;
And we are to the margin come,
    And soon must launch as they.

Our old companions in distress
    We haste again to see;
And eager long for our release,
    And full felicity.

E'en now by faith we join our hands
    With those that went before,
And great the blood-besprinkled bands
    On heaven's eternal shore.

Our spirits too shall quickly join,
    Like theirs with glory crowned;
And shout to see our Captain's sign,
    To hear His trumpet sound.

Oh, that we now might grasp our Guide,
    Oh, that the word were given!
Come, Lord of hosts! the waves divide,
    And land us all in heaven!

C. WESLEY

Also by J. C. Ryle

Five English Reformers

232pp., paperback
ISBN: 978 0 85151 138 2

Warnings to the Churches

176pp., paperback
ISBN: 978 0 85151 043 9

Thoughts for Young Men

96pp., paperback
ISBN: 978 1 84871 652 0

Also available in
eBook format from our website:

banneroftruth.org

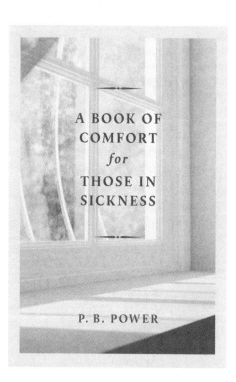

A BOOK OF
COMFORT
for
THOSE IN
SICKNESS

P. B. POWER

Also available from the Trust

A Book of Comfort for Those in Sickness
P. B. Power

Suffering need not be a dark experience …

While illness brings time to think, the natural tendency of our thoughts may not be comforting.

Sickness may end activities we once enjoyed; it will make us dependent upon others; and feelings of pain, or of usefulness, or of anxiety about the future, may be very real. To those who are in sickness the author does not underestimate the strength of those hindrances to comfort.

Far from offering superficial advice, P. B. Power's position in *A Book of Comfort for Those in Sickness* is that no comfort is obtainable unless there be, first, true knowledge of ourselves and, second, right knowledge of God.

His main aim is to state what this knowledge needs to be, and to show how with faith in God's character and presence, suffering need not be a dark experience.

112pp., paperback
ISBN: 978 1 84871 819 7

The Banner of Truth Trust originated in 1957 in London. The founders believed that much of the best literature of historic Christianity had been allowed to fall into oblivion and that, under God, its recovery could well lead not only to a strengthening of the church, but to true revival.

Inter-denominational in vision, this publishing work is now international, and our lists include a number of contemporary authors, together with classics from the past. The translation of these books into many languages is encouraged.

A monthly magazine, *The Banner of Truth*, is also published. More information about this and all our publications can be found on our website or supplied by either of the offices below.

THE BANNER OF TRUTH TRUST

3 Murrayfield Road
Edinburgh, EH12 6EL
UK

PO Box 621, Carlisle
Pennsylvania 17013
USA

bbanneroftruth.org